CANTON FOOTPRINTS

Sacramento's Chinese Legacy

BY PHILIP P. CHOY

CHINESE AMERICAN COUNCIL of SACRAMENTO

The officers and board members of the Chinese American Council of Sacramento would like to express their gratitude to Philip and Sarah Choy. Their selfless dedication to this project was inspirational. Their contribution to the preservation of Sacramento Chinese American history is greatly appreciated.

This book is dedicated to the Chinese pioneers whose shoulders we stand on; "they planted a tree so that we may enjoy the shade."

—Douglas and Karun Yee, *Book Committee Co-chairs / Research*

© 2007 Philip P. Choy. All rights reserved.
ISBN 978-1-60530-968-2

Chinese American Council of Sacramento
PO Box 22583
Sacramento, CA 95822

Book design by Gordon Chun Design
Printed in China through Global Interprint, Inc.

cover:
I Street, known to the Chinese as Tong Yun Gai (Chinese Street), circa 1880. (Courtesy of Sacramento Archives and Museum Collection Center)

frontispiece:
Diorama of Chinese Workers, California Railroad Museum, mural by artist Derrel Fleener (Courtesy of Malcolm Collier)

CONTENTS

The Chinese American Council Of Sacramento would like to acknowledge these Legacy Sponsors. Their generosity has made the publishing of this book possible.

THE CHAN FAMILY
General Produce

FRANK FAT FAMILY
In Memory of
FRANK, WING AND TOM FAT

In Honor of
PAUL ELWOOD FONG
Founder and CEO of Fong And Fong
Printers and Lithographers Inc.

In Loving Memory of Their Parents
MR. & MRS. SAM FONG
Audrey Ah Tye and Violet Chan
William, Edward and Roger Fong

The Quan Family in Memory of
MR. & MRS. GEORGE H. QUAN, SR.
James Quan, Henry Quan and
Dr. Georganne Quan

THE WONG FAMILY
Founders of the Bel Air Markets

In Memory of
DR. & MRS. HENRY W. YEE
Herbert and Inez Yee
Franklin and Sandra Yee

FOREWORD

As youngsters growing up in Chinatown, we frequently hear mention of Chinese American place names located in Northern California that are neither phonetically transcribed nor translated. These names often use San Francisco as the center or frame of reference: "We" live in Daai-fauh大埠 ("Big/First-seaport"); So-and-So Uncle lives in Ngee-fauh 二埠 ("Second-seaport"); So-and-So Uncle lives in Saam-fauh三埠 ("Third-seaport"), or So-and-So cousin lives in some fauh-jai 埠仔 ("Seaport-minor").

Those of us who grew up in San Francisco Chinatown hear these references so often that we take them for granted, without thinking why our early Chinese American ancestors have prioritized these Californian cities in such a hierarchical order. It was only years later that we come to understand that these place names have significant meaning for early Chinese American settlement history: San Francisco is the Big/First City (Daai-fauh) because it is the main port of entry and the center of Chinese American community activities since the early 1850s. From San Francisco, Chinese settlers branched out to other cities and towns. Sacramento is the Second City (Ngee-fauh, or Yee-fow for the Samyup dialect speakers) because of its pivotal role as a staging center to provide supply and service to the Chinese miners in the Mother Lode, the Chinese workers in the Transcontinental Railroad, and the Chinese farm workers in the Sacramento Delta. Chinese who live in Stockton, Marysville, and Oroville call their own city the Third City (Saamfauh or Sam Fow) because they believe that their city should rank third in importance in serving the Chinese labor recruited for agricultural land reclamation projects in the Sacramento Delta and San Joaquin Delta. Any other city or town, generally called the fauh-jai (or fauh-doi for Seiyup dialect speakers), just don't measure up to have a prioritized ranking of significance.[1] In fact, if one were to examine early California history since the 1850s, these three cities were the major population centers of early California, driving its political, social, and economic (financial, industrial, and agricultural) development activities to make the state what it is today. Thus, despite living in a segregated environment removed from mainstream California, the early Chinese Americans were cognizant of their participation and roles by appropriately calling these cities in such a hierarchical order.

Numerous academic and community publications have been devoted to the Chinese of America since Mary E. Coolidge's book, Chinese Immigration (1909). From Arnold Genthe to Him Mark Lai, there is plenty of comprehensive coverage on the Chinese in San Francisco. Sylvia Sun Minnick has published two books on Chinese in Stockton. Chinese Americans of Sacramento are like the neglected middle child in a family of three siblings. Other than a few writings paying tribute to local community figures, a more thorough study of the Sacramento Chinese is, unfortunately, long overdue. This present volume, a study of the formation of the Sacramento Chinese community by Philip P. Choy, fills this vacuum, especially in light of the fact that the Sacramento Chinese community, like the Los Angeles Chinatown in Southern California, has undergone quite a transformation in the last four decades. The once bustling Chinese ethnic enclave in downtown Sacramento has lost its close-knit community cohesiveness due to urban redevelopment.

In this book, Choy successfully links the development of the Sacramento Chinese American community to the larger framework of early Chinese American migration history, identifying in a balanced approach not just the formation of this Chinese community settlement, but also the central role it played in early Chinese American resettlement activities in Northern California. With well-documented references, Choy presents to the reader both a Sacramento Chinese community history, and a significant examination of the livelihood of the Chinese Americans who call Sacramento their home.

Choy has worn many hats: He is a self-employed architect now in retirement, enjoying time with his grandchildren. He is a pioneering educator who has teamed up with Him Mark Lai to teach the first-ever Chinese American history course at San Francisco State University in 1969. He is still an adjunct professor in its Asian American Studies Department despite being 80 years old. Choy is a community activist known for

landmark preservation in The City. He was a key member of the original China Cove Advisory Committee (for Angel Island Immigration Station restoration), and has always been a timely supporter and tireless volunteer for various community organizations like the Chinese Culture Center and especially for the Chinese Historical Society of America (CHSA), involving himself with numerous projects and activities, exhibitions, and capital campaigns. He is also known as a Chinese American archivist, a clearinghouse of information, who has generously offered his reservoir of knowledge and resources to researchers of Chinese American history and culture without reservation, allowing the latter to make use of his resources for their books and films without even concern for his own proprietary ownership. The listing of his selflessness goes on and on, and is too long to be detailed here.

What is most impressive is Choy's devotion and dedication to research, preserve, advocate, and disseminate Chinese American history. He does so, not for tenure and promotion in the academe, or for name and fame in the community. He has traveled as far as the Guangdong and Jiejiang provinces of China to search for old kilns in hopes of identifying a common linkage to the potteries, bowls, and dishes he found at excavation sites of old California chinatowns. More important, Choy's activities and actions are always of pioneering quality. He was the first to make a video documentary series called the

Gum Saan Haak on Chinese American history for public broadcasting. He was the first to stand firm and publicly challenge the organizers of the 1969 Transcontinental Railroad Centennial at Promontory Point to acknowledge the Chinese participation in the construction of the Transcontinental Railroad in the 1860s, thus reclaiming the recognition of Chinese railroad workers whose contributions and sacrifices in this nation-building project had been neglected for a century. Choy was there when the San Francisco Chinese community organized and prepared the Angel Island Immigration Station exhibit as Barrack 37 opened to the public, allowing us to better understand the forgotten history of this so-called Ellis Island of the West during the dark period of Chinese exclusion. Choy worked with associates and brought to light the buried past of the Chinese Camp in Tuolumne County, revealing the once common presence of the Chinese in the Sierra foothills of an earlier era. He volunteered his time and resource to put the CHSA Chinese American history exhibits together as the CHSA headquarters moved from place to place from Adler Alley, to Commercial Street, Broadway Street, and finally to Clay Street.

This is Phil Choy's passion, searching for the history of the Chinese in California. He has been doing this since the 1960s. One can still imagine, in the mid-1980s, Phil and his wife Sarah in their brand new, bright red two-seater sports car, cruising up and down the California coast and the foothills of the Sierra in search of Chinese American settlement camps and communities far and near, past and present. Choy's field-based research represents an aspect of research where many of us have failed to do, let alone to do it with such dedication, vigor, and automotive style. Of course, we all wish to have such class and elegance to carry out our research and field study activities.

This present volume on the Sacramento Chinese is Choy's latest effort to provide the best evidentiary testimony to reclaim Chinese America's legacy in California. It has definitely provided new insight on Sacramento Chinatown, the "neglected middle child" of the Chinese community.

Marlon K. Hom

Professor and Chair
Asian American Studies Department
San Francisco State University
May, 2007

Notes:
1. According to Choy, the old mill town of Hanford was once known among early Chinese settlers as Ngh-fauh 五埠 ("Fifth-seaport"). To date, no reference to a Sei-fauh 四埠 ("Fourth-seaport") can be found. Apparently, Chinese communities do not want to be known as Sei-fauh, since the word sei or "four" is culturally taboo in Cantonese because it is a homonym for sei 死 or "death." Chinese residents in both Stockton and Marysville had no problem claiming their hometown as Saam-fauh, as saam 三 or "three" in Cantonese is similar in sound to saang 生 or "live/birth/grow."

No. 621

CERTIFICATE FOR MERCHANT.

TO ALL TO WHOM THESE PRESENTS MAY COME.

GREETING!

This is to certify that *Ao Yeong Hung Hing* to whom this certificate is issued and who is about to go to the United States, is a subject of His Imperial Chinese Majesty the Emperor of China, and is hereby permitted and entitled under the provisions of the Act of Congress of the United States of America, entitled "An Act to execute certain Treaty stipulations relating to Chinese, Approved May 6th 1882, as amended July 5th, 1884, "and the Treaty between the United States of America and China, dated November 17th, 1880, to go within the United States of America upon presentation of this certificate to the Collector of Customs of the Port in the District of the United States at which he shall arrive.

The individual, family and tribal name in full of said permitted person is,

Individual Hing family Hung Tribal 歐陽鴻興

The following is the name of such permitted person in his own proper signature,

His title or official rank is _____

His age is *24 years.*   His height is *5 feet 7½*

His physical peculiarities are *scar on left ear & on right side of nose*

His former occupation was that of *dealer in general M'dise* pursued in

Heong Shan City during the years *1899 to 1900,*

His present occupation is that of *dealer in genl Merchandise* doing business

and trading in *Wo King Lee Street Canton*

under the name of *Kwong Allow Lung* said firm having a capital $ *8,000,*

and this applicant's interest therein being $ *3000,* That said business has been

pursued in *Canton* for *three* years, His place of residence

has been in Lin Hong Village Heong Shan Dist. China

Issued by the Imperial Government of China at the Office of the Superintendent of the Imperial Customs at Canton. In witness whereof, I have hereunto set my hand and affixed the seal of my Office on the *22nd* day of *April*, 1904

常晨 Seong   Yan,

Superintendent of Imperial Customs, Canton

I do hereby certify that I have examined into the truth of the statements set forth in the foregoing certificate, and find upon examination that the same are true. That the seal and signature to the foregoing certificate are the genuine seal and signature of the duly qualified and acting Superintendent of the Imperial Customs of the Imperial Government of China at Canton.

In witness whereof, I have hereunto set my hand and affixed the seal of this Consulate at Canton, China, on the *10th* day of *May* 1904

Fee.... $1.00 Gold

Robert M. Mc Wade

United States Consul General.

Impression Rt. mid finger

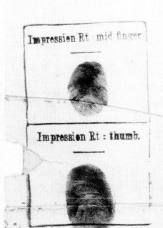

Impression Rt : thumb.

Merchant Certificate of Hing Hung Owyang
(Courtesy of Al Yuen)

INTRODUCTION

The discovery of gold in California is generally accepted as the lure for Chinese immigration to the United States. Likewise, the Opium War, Taiping Revolution, flood, famine, pirates, and banditry are considered to have precipitated emigration from China to other parts of the world. Accepting these theories without attention to the two hundred years of intricate socio-economic, political, and religious intrigue between Asia and America that predated the gold rush, perpetuates the myth that in the late nineteenth and early twentieth centuries the Chinese came primarily because America was the "land of the free."

From its birth as a new nation, America competed with European nations in search of trade with China. The obsession with taking advantage of the wealth of the Far East was a major stimulus to western expansion to the Pacific Coast. The acquisition of Washington, Oregon, and California established a gateway to the Pacific without the arduous and seemingly endless journey around Cape Hope. In the process, pioneers explored and developed the country in their westward journey to the coast.

Along with merchants seeking tea, silk, and porcelain, missionaries of the American evangelical movement marched into the Pacific Islands, Southeast Asia, and China, crusading "the noblest course on earth." After two centuries of trading and religious intervention, conflict ensued, and the demands of the West began to undermine China's

sovereignty. The Manchu (also known as the Qing) government was not able to stem the tide of imperialism of the western nations, and China was reduced to a semicolonial state. A vast pool of desperate laborers became available to satisfy the world's labor needs.

At the same time that China's unemployed masses were looking for work, European nations needed laborers to exploit the resources of their newly conquered colonies spread throughout the globe. Thus, well before the discovery of gold in California, the Chinese had already signed labor contracts under which they were shipped all over the world in what became known as the "Coolie Trade."

The availability of a vast pool of Chinese labor was perfectly timed to the needs of the developing new state of California. In addition to searching for gold, the Chinese found work in clearing the swampland in the Sacramento River Delta, in agriculture, and in building the railroads. Sacramento, second only to San Francisco in population and importance, was the gateway to the northern mines. The Chinese first settled in Sacramento to serve the Chinese miners, and subsequently to serve the laborers in the development of the delta region.

The trade with China and the greed for profit from transporting human cargo stimulated America's need for fast ships, thus fostering the development of American commercial maritime power—power that eventually rivaled, challenged, and finally surpassed that of perennial sea power Britain. Historians gaze back to Europe for America's roots and heritage. However, our nation's sights toward the Pacific not so long after the War of Independence led to exploration across the continent. That impetus resulted in events that led to the discovery of gold, and the coming of the Chinese to California.

As the frontier matured and more people came west, the Chinese ran into competition with an emerging white laboring class. Caught between the nation's struggle between labor versus capital, the Chinese became scapegoats for the growing pains of the American labor movement in the western United States.

The immigration of the Chinese may be divided into three time periods: 1) From the beginning of the gold rush to the Exclusion Act of 1882, during which time thousands of Chinese participated in the development of the West; 2) from the exclusion era between 1882 and 1943, during which time thousands of Chinese were denied their "inalienable rights"; and, 3) from 1943, when the Chinese were allowed to become citizens, to the present when Chinese immigration is treated on an equal basis with all other nations.

AUTHOR'S NOTE

Federal regulations mandate archeological surveys be conducted on sites used for federal buildings. The HI56 block in Sacramento was selected for the new federal courthouse. The deposits recovered by archeologists, Mary & Adrian Praetzellis from the Anthropological Studies Center, Sonoma State University, found the site to be where the Chinese had settled in 1852. The Chinese American Council of Sacramento (CACS) cooperated with federal authorities on the installation of a permanent exhibit in the lobby. I was the project director. Subsequently I accepted the proposal by Dr. Douglas Yee of CACS to write the history of the Chinese of Sacramento.

To gather material for the book, CACS published requests for Chinese Sacramentans to come forth and be interviewed. To those that responded, I'm especially appreciative of your openness and integrity and for entrusting me with your personal family histories: Audrey Fong Ah Tye, Daniel W. Chan, Edward Chan, Virginia Fong Chan, Rollana M. Chong, Paul Dong, Wing Kai Fat, William "Bill" Fong, Edna Mae Fong, M.D., Ella C. Fong, Elizabeth Fong, Florence Fong, Harold Fong, Joe S. Fong, Joe Wayne Fong, Mae Lum Fong, Paul Fong, Raymond G. Fong, Robert W. H. Fong, Roger Fong, Wallace Fong, William Wei Yee Fong, Yen Fong, Elizabeth F. Fung, Ruby Yuke Fung, Melvin Hing, Tim Jang, Ping K. Lee, Raymond Lee, Jim Y. Louie, (Mah) Lien Ung Lum, Marion Chin Ono, Helen Fong Owyang, Dr. Hing

Owyang, Jr., George Quan, Jr., Ronald Tom, Merrily Fong Wong, Bill Wong, George R. Wong, Franklin Yee, M.D., Dr. Herbert K. Yee, Jimmie R. Yee, Joyce J. Yee, Philip Hong Yee, Rose Yee, Bennie Woon Yep, Mary Yip.

Doug and Karun Yee of CACS, who were the spirit behind the project, dedicated much of their time contacting and scheduling the interviews. Karun chauffeured me on and off Interstate 5. I had every confidence she would out bluff truck drivers who got in her way. Karun also videotaped the sessions.

In addition to those interviewed, I wish to acknowledge the following persons for providing me with additional resources and assistance: Dr. Florence J. Chinn, Rollana M. Chong, Carol Jan Lee, Russell N. Low, Margaret (Dong) Lum, and Al Yuen for permission to quote from their journals and biographies, Dr. Franklin K. Yee for allowing me to quote from his essay on the Chinese in the medical field, Alex Eng for material on the contemporary Asian community, Pat Johnson, Carson Hendriks, and Dillion McDonald, the staff at Sacramento Archives and Museum Collection Center, Yuet Ho Tsui for translating Chinese language material, including the titles, Him Mark Lai for sharing his Chinese material, Carolyn Chinn Hung, Marcia Chan, Bruce Quan, Jr. for making contacts for me with their family members, and Anna Naruta for locating the article on John Jan.

I would like to thank Jeanie Yee, Florence

Fong and Douglas and Karun Yee for spending meticulous hours proofreading the manuscript, catching typographical errors such as "gum boats" in lieu of "gun boats."

Over the forty years of my work on projects dealing with the subject of the Chinese of America, my family has given me unstinting support. Because of my imbedded Chinese humbleness "not to boast of family," I have never acknowledged them publicly. It's time I give credit long overdue. As always, I've depended on my son Randy and daughter Stephanie for editing and proofreading the manuscript and giving me input. My photographer son Brian and his multi-skilled wife Victoria saved CACS thousands of dollars by creating the electronic file for book designer, Gordon Chun. In addition, Victoria proofread the manuscript. The latest addition to this family spirit, my grandson Michael Choy assisted me with computer graphic work. Finally, my wife Sarah doggedly attempted to keep pace with the 20th century by using word perfect to type and re-type the manuscript without complaints except with an occasional outburst . . . "ai-ye-aah!!. I'm too old for this!!" It's a minor miracle she still cooks my dinner.

It is my loss that I knew Anna Wong Lee only briefly. In our few meetings, her love and passion for the community she grew up in was contagious. Her untimely death left a void in the knowledge of the Chinese community, but her collection deposited with the Sacramento Archives and Museum Collection Center insures she will be remembered as the custodian-historian of the Chinese of Sacramento.

Standard romanization of the Chinese language "pinyin" did not exist until after 1949. Since the setting of this book is in the United States and the emigrants to Sacramento prior to 1949 were pre-dominantly from the Pearl River Delta in Guangdong Province known as the Cantonese, their names are maintained in the Cantonese dialect with their place of origin in Cantonese followed by pinyin in parenthesis. Since the proper names of Chinese are often times identical, the maiden surnames of married females are inserted with parenthesis. The names of famous people, places and major events in history used in pre-1949 writings are maintained, but at the discretion of the author may be followed by pinyin in parenthesis.

This book is not intended to be a biography of people who made history in the Chinese community, but rather it is the story of how the events of history impacted people and led to the evolution of a community. The knowledge of events placed in historical context validates our existence in Gum Saan (America).

Philip P. Choy
2007

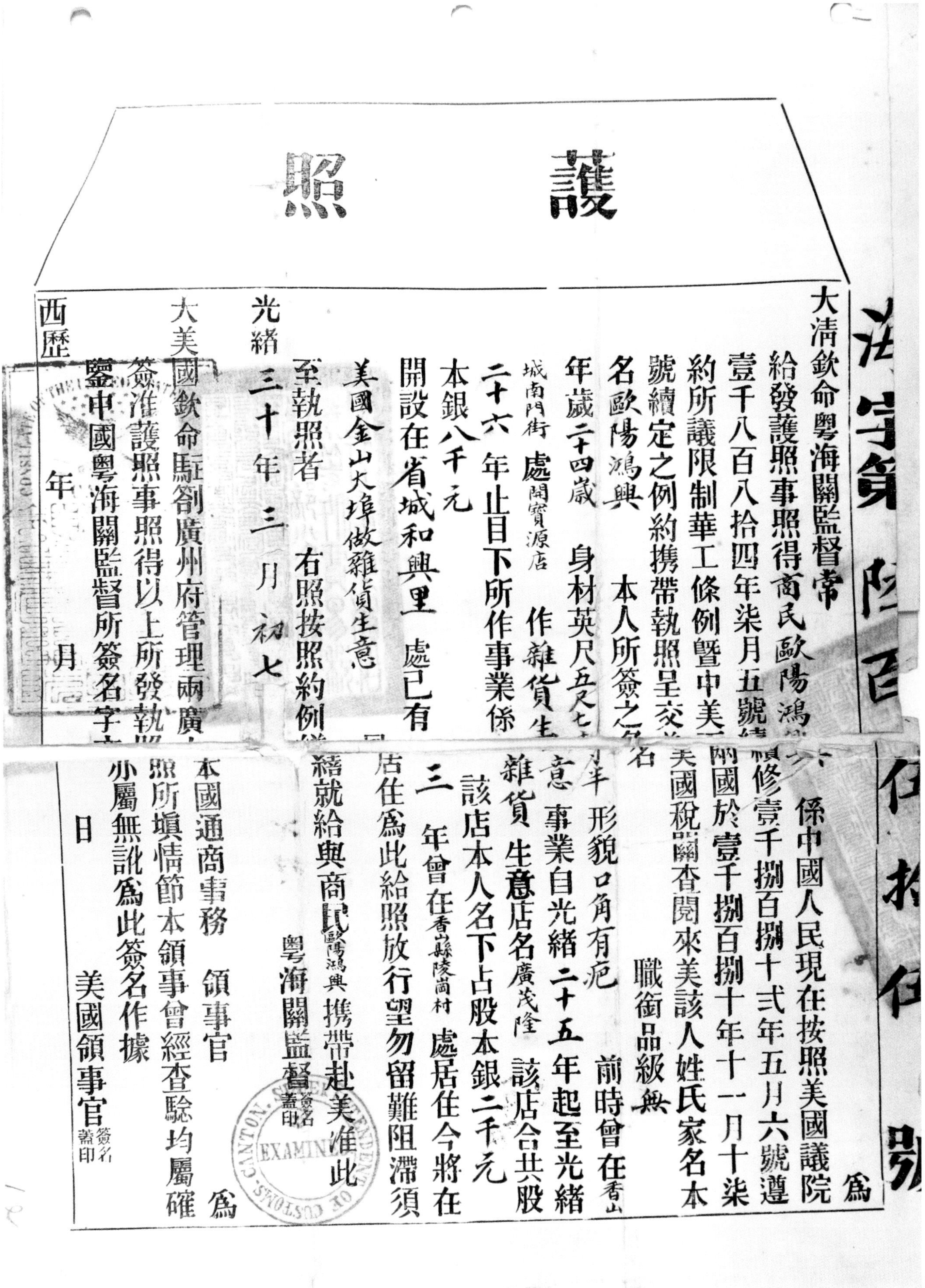
護照

法字第陸百伍拾伍號

大清欽命粵海關監督常　爲
給發護照事照得商民歐陽鴻興係中國人民現在按照美國議院
壹千八百八拾四年柒月五號續修壹千捌百捌十弍年五月六號遵
約所議限制華工條例暨中美兩國於壹千捌百捌十年十一月十柒
號續定之例約携帶執照呈交美國稅關查閱來美該人姓氏家名本
名歐陽鴻興　本人所簽之名　職銜品級無
年歲二十四歲　身材英尺五尺七寸半　形貌口角有疤　前時曾在香山
城南門街處開寶源店作雜貨生意事業自光緒二十五年起至光緒
二十六年止目下所作事業係雜貨生意店名廣茂隆　該店合共股
本銀八千元　該店本人名下占股本銀二千元
開設在省城和興里　處已有三　年曾在香山縣陵尚村　處居住今將在
美國金山大埠做雜貨生意居住爲此給照放行望勿留難阻滯須
至執照者　右照按照約例繕就給與商民歐陽鴻興携帶赴美准此
粵海關監督　簽名蓋印
光緒三十年三月初七
大美國欽命駐劄廣州府管理兩廣本國通商事務　領事官　爲
簽准護照事照得以上所發執照所塡情節本領事會經查驗均屬確
鑒中國粵海關監督所簽名字亦屬無訛爲此簽名作據
西歷　年　月　日
美國領事官　簽名蓋印

Merchant Certificate of Hing Hung Owyang in Chinese
(Courtesy of Al Yuen)

The fascination with which the West once viewed China in the 18th century had deteriorated to disrespect and disdain in the 19th century.

Foreign factories outside the Canton city wall where foreigners stayed and conducted trade. 1815. L to R, Austrian, American, British and Dutch flags flying in front of their respective factories.

PART I

DISINTEGRATION OF THE MANCHU EMPIRE

滿清滅亡

In the years 1833–1834, 254 vessels arrived at Whampoa. Of those vessels, 101 were British and 70 were American. (Author's collection)

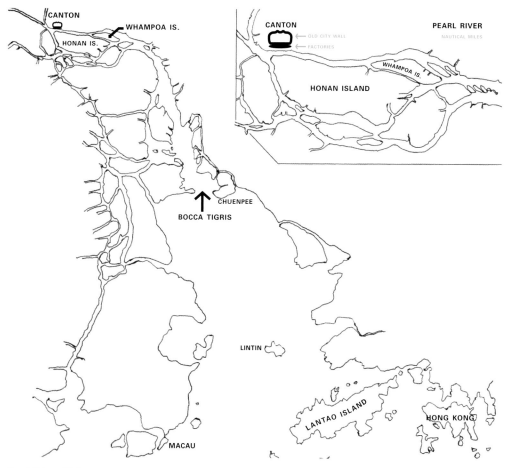

Pearl River Delta

CHAPTER ONE

America and the Far East

When Europeans encountered China in the late 1600s during the Ming dynasty, China was self-sufficient and looked upon herself as a civilization advanced far beyond that of Europe. China needed little from the "inferior civilizations," whereas Europe was fascinated and entranced with the "Middle Kingdom" and coveted her luxuries. By the beginning of the eighteenth century, the mania for Chinese culture had swept across Europe. Chinese motifs dominated design in architecture and in landscape, and became known as the rococo style. Men wore coats, vests, and trousers, and women wore gowns, all fashioned from Chinese silk. Tea from China was served in porcelain teacups. Porcelain dinnerware and silverware were placed upon tablecloths of Chinese fabric—and all were made to order, and imported from China.

Chinese luxury goods impacted the culture of the colonies in the New World as well. New World trade was still dependent on British merchants and British ships. The heavy taxation of Chinese tea on the colonies was the impetus for revolt and ultimately mushroomed into the American war for independence. Following the Revolutionary War of 1776, the fledgling nation immediately entered into competition with European nations in the struggle to dominate commerce in the Far East. China trade was deemed essential to the economy of the newly-founded United States of America.

In 1784, the first American ship, *Empress of China,* sailed through the Bocca Tigris (Humen) and announced her arrival with a thirteen-gun salute to honor the European vessels anchored at Whampoa. Each vessel in return welcomed the newcomer with a one-gun salute.[1] Canton lay fourteen miles upstream where the "hong" merchants were authorized by the Chinese government to conduct and regulate trade with the foreigners at a designated area known as the "thirteen factories." At the factories, the young nation hoisted the Stars and Stripes alongside seasoned European traders, the Dutch, British, Swedes, Belgians, French, and Danes.

The Chinese referred to the Americans as the "New People"[2] from the country of the "Fah Kay" (Flowery Flag), and her major commodity for trade was Fah Kay ginseng, which was highly valued by the Chinese for its medicinal properties. After trading more than twenty-eight tons of ginseng and twenty thousand Spanish silver dollars and some minor items, the *Empress of China* returned to New York on May 11, 1785, with a cargo of tea, silk, porcelain, cinnamon bark, and other treasures. Major Samuel Shaw, the supercargo of the *Empress of China* wrote in his journal, "The inhabitants of America must have tea, the consumption of which will necessarily increase with the population of our country."[3]

SAMUEL SHAW

The resounding financial success of this

VIEW OF SOUTH STREET, NEW YORK CITY.

The seaports of New York City, Boston, and Philadelphia became synonymous with Canton, Macao, and Shanghai. (Author's collection)

voyage created a mania for chinoiserie. For over six decades, Chinese import goods impacted New England's household culture. Not only tea, silk, and porcelain were imported, but the well-appointed New England household also exhibited manufactured goods made with the ingenuity and craftsmanship of the Chinese artisan. Leather trunks, furniture of Chippendale, Empire, and Greek Revival designs, secretaries, sewing tables, fabrics, and floor coverings were all Chinese manufactured and decorated American households.

Until 1789, ships sailing for the Far East followed the *Empress of China's* formula for success by crossing the Atlantic and rounding Cape Hope with a cargo of ginseng as the major commodity for trade with China.

In 1787, the *Lady Washington,* captained by Robert Grey, and the *Columbia,* captained by John Kendrick, sailed by way of Cape Horn up the coast to the Pacific Northwest and thence westward across the Pacific to the Far East. These traders traveled through the Pacific Northwest seeking fur as a substitute for ginseng. Ironware, hatchets, knives, chisels, firearms and powder, mirrors, beads, and cloth were bartered with Native Americans for pelts and seal skins. The fur trade was supplemented with other items in demand by the Chinese that were found on the islands of the Pacific: Sandalwood from Hawaii was used in the temples as incense; and bech-de-mar (sea cucumber) was a delicacy eaten by the Chinese. On his second trip to the Pacific Northwest in 1792, Captain Grey discovered the Columbia River. At that time there were

白地五彩描金帆船酒盌 清 乾隆

清 嘉慶 藍褐彩鷹徽茶壺（銷美國）

Besides porcelain with purely Chinese designs, orders for complete sets of dinner service were made with patterns of family crests and coat of arms.

純正 100% PURE 花旗蔘茶 AMERICAN GINSENG TEA NET WT 1.6 oz 528oz

Contemporary packaging of ginseng still uses the original Chinese term "fah kay" (flowery flag) for America.

(Courtesy of Dan Tom)

The Empress of China's outward bound cargo for China was twenty-eight tons of ginseng and twenty thousand Spanish silver dollars.

Ginseng, sea otter fur, seal skins, sandalwood, and sea cucumber were major articles of trade with China.

twenty-one vessels along the Northwest coast, most of which were owned by Americans.

When John Jacob Astor entered the China trade in 1808, he sailed the *Beaver* along the Northwest coast, and established the first American trading post, which he named Astoria. The rise in fortune of the cities of Salem, Boston, Baltimore, Providence, Philadelphia, and New York, and the emergence of the ship building industry in New England, was a direct response to the need for faster and larger ships to facilitate trade with China. The activities of captains Robert Grey, John Astor, and others were the basis of the United States' claims to the vast Northwest territory that is now Oregon and Washington.

SOLDIERS OF THE CROSS

While British and American merchants opened the doors to the treasure house of the Middle Kingdom, European and Anglo American missionaries envisioned opening the doors to yet three hundred million more souls to enter the kingdom of God. Canton soon became the staging area for Protestant missionary enterprises.

At the beginning of the nineteenth century, a Protestant religious revival movement known as the Second Great Awakening fostered a missionary spirit bent on evangelizing the "heathen" world. This religious movement inspired the founding of the London Missionary Society (LMS) and the American Board of Commissioners of Foreign Missions.

The first Protestant missionary, Rev. Robert Morrison, was appointed by the LMS in 1807. The first American missionaries, Rev. Elijah Bridgman and Rev. David Abeel III, were appointed by the American Board.

The United States Government had not prepared anyone for diplomatic service and therefore depended on the missionaries for assistance. Missionaries became official representatives of the United States and were appointed as diplomats or consular officers.[4] As such they influenced early policies made between China and the United States. For nearly four decades from the time the *Empress of China* arrived in China, American merchants depended on Rev. Robert Morrison for translation and interpretation until in 1830, the American missionary Rev. Elijah Bridgman arrived and he spoke Cantonese. Samuel Wells Williams arrived in 1833. He was a printer and a convert, not an ordained minister. Rev. Peter Parker, a medical missionary, arrived in 1834. Parker had learned Cantonese from seventeen-year-old Ah Leong, who lived with Samuel Russell, a retired merchant from the China trade.

In negotiating the Treaty of Wanghia (1844), Bridgman and Parker were interpreters and advisors to Commissioner Caleb Cushing, a member of the Committee on Foreign Affairs, appointed by President John Tyler, to head the legation. Parker became the official interpreter and secretary to the legation; likewise, Williams was the interpreter for the Tientsin Treaty (1858) and remained for twenty years in the service of the legation.

CHAPTER TWO

Western Imperialism and Internal Disorder

Trade was conducted at the ports of Macao (Aomen), Canton (Guangzhou), Amoy (Xiamen), Ningpo (Ningbo), and Foochow (Fuzhou) under strict and burdensome Chinese regulations. For example, the foreign traders were required to pay for their goods in silver. Their constant protesting of unfair and irregular practices and heavy duties caused the Emperor Ch'ien Lung (Qian-long) in 1757 to limit trading only to the port of Canton. As competition became intense, the restriction of trade to the thirteen factories under the control of government officials, known as hongs, became unacceptable to the western powers competing for greater access to China.

BRITISH AND AMERICAN OPIUM TRADE

The demand to trade in silver caused a trade deficit among foreign nations. A commodity was needed to offset the imbalance. The answer, unfortunately, was opium. The British, in an effort to extend their commercial markets, increased the smuggling of opium into China. Americans took part in the trade in as early as 1805, obtaining the opium from Smyrna, Turkey. At the beginning of foreign trade, China's exports exceeded her imports.

With the introduction of opium as a medium of exchange, this situation soon changed.

The increased importation of smuggled opium, now ironically paid for in silver by the Chinese, reversed the balance of trade and undermined China's economy. Emperor Tao Kuang (Dao Guang, 1821–1851) subsequently issued an edict to prohibit the import of opium. The British ignored the edict and openly continued to import the illicit drug. China's determined efforts to stop the opium trade led to open warfare as the British traders refused to relinquish their advantage. However, China's antiquated weapons and undisciplined troops were no match for

While British merchants were shipping opium for the pipes of China, British evangelist Rev. Robert Morrison was preaching the gospel to the Chinese.

(Courtesy of Brian Choy)

The fleet of about fifteen Chinese war junks were destroyed by the British warship Nemesis at Chuenpee. 1841. (Author's collection)

China's antiquated weapons and undisciplined troops were no match for the Queen's warships.

Signing the Treaty of Nanking in the State Cabin of H.M. Ship Cornwallis. 1842. (Author's collection)

the Queen's warships, and the war ended in China's surrender.

Defeated in the Opium War (1839-1842), China was forced to open the ports of Canton, Shanghai, Ningpo, Amoy, and Foochow to trade. China ceded away rights to western nations to maintain colonies at treaty ports, and reluctantly granted extraterritorial rights. Hong Kong was ceded to England for one hundred years. Foreign citizens in China were no longer subject to the laws of China, but to the laws of their own countries. Protected by modern gunboats, merchants and their ships could now sail freely on the waterways of China.

The United States took part in the imperialist movement and insisted on the same privileges granted the other countries. The fascination with which the West once viewed China in the eighteenth century had deteriorated to disrespect and disdain in the nineteenth century. The Chinese were ridiculed as an effete and dying civilization. China under the Manchu rulers was indeed on the verge of collapse. Government corruption, socioeconomic dislocation, and sectarian rebellion were factors in the demise of the Qing. Western powers continued to exploit China's weakness, and ultimately partitioned China into their own individual spheres of interest.

With the signing of the Treaty of Nanking (1842) began the semicolonization of China by foreign powers and the beginning of the end of 267 years of Manchu (1644–1911) reign over China. The foreign policy of the Manchu government was one of appeasement, continually granting concessions in response to the demands of foreign nations. As a consequence, the important ports along the China coast came under foreign control, which dictated the terms of customs and tariffs. The corruption, depravity, and ineptness of the Manchu bureaucracy made it unable to deal with the belligerent lust of the western

The United States took part in the imperialist movement and insisted on the same privileges granted to other nations.

The Treaty of Wang-Hea (Wanghia) between China and America was signed on July 3, 1844, at a round stone table in the temple garden in Wanghia, Macao. (Courtesy of Marlon Hom)

nations. Anti-Manchu resentment among the native population began to fester.

TAIPING REBELLION (1851–1864)

Nine years after the Treaty of Nanking, the country experienced a tremendous peasant uprising known as the Taiping Rebellion. The Taiping's revolutionary ideology borrowed from Protestant Christianity then forming in Canton. Robert Morrision, the first Protestant evangelist who came to Canton in 1807, had translated the Bible into Chinese. His convert, Liang Afa, was responsible for producing the booklet entitled *Good Words to Admonish the Age*. The works of these two evangelists influenced the development of the Taiping religious ideology.

A Hakka peasant schoolteacher named Hong Xiuquan led the uprising. Hong was an aspiring civil servant from Hua-hsien, Guangdong, who failed several attempts to pass the civil service exams. Passing the exams meant bringing fame, glory, and fortune for himself, his family, and the village. The humiliation of his failure was so great that Hong suffered a nervous breakdown. During his illness he had delirious hallucinations of an old man giving him a sword and instructing him to slay demons. Years later, recovering from his illness, he took the civil service exam and failed again. Upon returning home the disgruntled and disappointed Hong rediscovered the religious tracts passed out by Liang Afa when Hong first arrived in Canton to take his examination. Hong read the material and experienced an epiphany. He interpreted the visions he had seen during his illness as a message from God, instructing him to establish the heavenly kingdom on earth to fight evil. Jesus Christ was instructing him as his older brother, and he, Hong, was also the son of God. Subsequently, he spent two months in Canton with American Southern Baptist missionary Rev. Issachar J. Roberts to further his knowledge of Christian doctrine. Hong developed his own interpretation of the Bible,

Taiping rebels with reinforcement skirmish against Manchu troops.

SECOND OPIUM WAR (1856–1860)

Taking advantage of the Manchu government's turmoil with the Taiping rebels and dissatisfied with the treaties made in 1842, both the British and French resolved to extract further concessions from China. Using minor incidents as excuses, a second opium war broke out. A Chinese-owned ship the *Arrow* with a Chinese crew sailing under the protection of the British flag was seized by Chinese authorities for smuggling. The British, protesting the hauling down of the flag as an insult, took military action. A French missionary was murdered so France sent troops to join the British. The Anglo-French allied armies attacked Canton in 1857 and thereafter had military control of the city for three years. Under the 1858 Treaty of Tientsin, trading of opium became legal. Protected by modern gunboats, foreign merchants and their ships sailed freely on the waterways of China.

". . . its government is engaged in a two-front strife, with its own rebels and with the might of England."

Ballou's Pictorial, May 9, 1857

Prayer and blessings before going into battle against the Chinese at Canton. (Author's collection)

adding and deleting elements of the scripture, fusing it with Chinese ideas and traditions to suit his own religious ideas. Under Hong, the Taiping troops were required to attend religious services, pray to God, and memorize the Ten Commandments.

For fifteen years the Taiping army battled the Manchu troops, bringing turmoil to eighteen provinces in south and central China. The Taiping Rebellion resulted in the deaths of more than twenty million people.

PUNTI AND HAKKA FEUD

The population of Guangdong consisted mainly of two groups: the Punti and the Hakka. The earliest settlers of the province called themselves Punti (indigenous settlers) and euphemistically labeled the later emigrants as Hakka (guest families meaning outsiders). Each group settled in their own villages and maintained their own customs and language. Friction and feuding were common between the two, often erupting in small scale warfare. In the Pearl River Delta, a half million people were killed in the clashes.

Accelerating the decline of China's economy and the deterioration of social conditions in Guangdong were widespread banditry, piracy, rebellious activities of secret societies, uncontrolled population growth, and foreign exploitation.

In Guangdong, eight thousand followers of bandit chiefs Ta Li-Yu (Great Carp) and Ta-Tou Yang (Big Head Ram) plundered freely without inference from local authorities. From 1762 to the time of the first opium war in 1841, the population more than doubled from 200,472,261 to 413,457,311.

MASS EMIGRATION

Contemporaneous with events of rebellion in China was a worldwide evangelical Protestant crusade, the Second Great Awakening, which spirited the emancipation of the African slave trade. While perhaps noble in intent, the crusade fomented a shortage of cheap labor. The economic dislocation of the Chinese in Guangdong Province filled this void and made available a seemingly inexhaustible reservoir of cheap labor to replace slavery. This became known as "the coolie trade," as evil as the African slave trade. Beginning in the 1840s, hundreds of thousands of Chinese were kidnapped and carried off, mainly in British and American vessels, to all parts of the world: to the sugar plantations in Cuba and Hawaii; to the tin mines and rubber plantations in Southeast Asia; to harvest the guano deposits in the Chincha Islands off the coast of Peru; to the islands of Maritius and Madagascar off the east coast of Africa. The sometimes involuntary Chinese diaspora extended the Chinese population throughout the world even before the discovery of gold in California.

The decline of China under the Manchu government was also contemporaneous with the westward expansion of America, which ultimately led to the discovery of gold in California. Not only were the Chinese attracted to the gold fields of California, the abundance of cheap Chinese labor became a resource by which California was to be developed. Affected by foreign intervention and exploitation, people from Guangdong formed the first major ranking of immigrants to the United States. The coming of the Chinese to Sacramento is a microcosm of this mass emigration.

Chinese Emigration.

The following table, compiled with great care, from memorandas kept by S. E. Woodworth, Esq., exhibits the number of Chinese who have arrived at this port since the 1st day of January, 1852, from China and other ports in the Pacific. It will be seen that the entire number is 18,040. The number that have sailed since May 1st, 1852, is 71—thus leaving the number of 17,969 remaining in the country. Strange to say, of the above immense emigration, there are only 14 women, the majority of whom are in this city at the present time. The number is disproportionately small, taking into consideration the length of time that many of them have been in California. It would appear as if those who had returned to the Celestial Empire, had no other object in view but to advise their brethren to come.

Alta California
August 13, 1852

		Names of Vessels	Nation			
March	1	B'rq William Walton	British		61	226
"	12	B'rq John Mayo	American		73	135
"	25	Ship Henbury	British		62	230
"	25	B'rq Frederick Bohm	Prussian		73	129
"	29	Ship North Carolina	American		59	356
April	9	B'rq Ann Welsh			49	152
"	11	B'rq Emperor	British		68	181
"	11	B'rq Glenlyon			71	150
"	12	B'rq George Washington	Bremen		56	196
"	20	B'rq Ternate	Dutch		61	263
"	21	Sh p Blenheim	British		59	346
"	22	Ship Challenge	American		34	553
"	24	Brig Nicholas Nicholson	Norweg'n		63	100
"	28	Ship Constant	British		78	250
May	1	Ship Brahmin			57	286
"	1	B'rq Sophie	Portug'se	Macao	62	164
"	7	Ship Rajasthan	British	Hongkong	55	320
"	11	Ship Robert Small			52	372
"	15	Ship Witchcraft	American		44	344
"	22	Brig Reindeer	Hawaiian	Shanghai	40	4
"	23	Ship Grace McVea	British	Macao	84	336
June	1	Brig Copiapo	Mexican	Mazatlan	34	7
"	2	B'rq Palmetto	American	Shanghai	45	47
"	3	Ship Amity		Whampoa	69	293
"	3	Ship Balmoral	British		51	464
"	4	B'rq Queen		Macao	63	252
"	4	Ship Gilbert	Bremen	Hongkong	49	285
"	5	Ship Ville de Tonniers	French		58	340
"	6	Ship Sir George Pollock	British		50	310
"	8	Ship Exchange	American		53	258
"	9	Ship Iowa	Peruvian		54	379
"	10	B'rq Daniel Ross	Hamburg		67	212
"	11	Ship Emily Taylor	American		53	224
"	14	B'rq Walter Morrice	British		49	336
"	15	B'rq Aurora			55	234
"	17	B'rq Eden		Macao	61	348
"	19	Ship Monsoon		Hongkong	58	494
"	25	Ship Acadia			65	287
"	26	B'rq Ann Martin			65	255
"	28	B'rq Sarah Hooper			60	86
"	28	Ship Eliza Morrison			65	410
"	28	Brig Lombock	Danish		62	103
"	30	Ship William Money	British		61	502
July	3	B'rq Cornwall			60	178
"	4	B'rq Anna	Dutch	Macao	60	178
"	5	B'rq Augusta	British	Hongkong	64	242
"	5	Ship Duke of Northumb'd			66	358
"	5	Ship Akbar			58	377
"	6	Ship Viceroy		Macao	53	358
"	19	Ship Sobraon		Hongkong	52	63
"	19	Brig Emma	Bremen		76	130
"	19	B'rq Louisiana	American		66	166
"	20	Ship Lord Weston	British		64	293
"	20	B'rq Linda	Equador	Macao	60	55
"	20	B'rq Essex	British	Hongkong	70	193
"	22	Ship Baron Renfrew			63	580
"	22	B'rq Ohio	American	Macao	90	204
"	27	B'rq Ella Francis		Hongkong	74	210
"	28	B'rq Ocean Queen	British	Macao	77	466
Aug.	1	Ship Sultan		Hongkong	43	427
"	1	Ship Far West	American		52	343
"	1	Ship Amoy	British		51	391
"	1	Ship Lady Amherst			50	263
"	2	Ship Troubadour			47	476
"	4	B'rq Dragon	American		52	20
"	6	B'rq Emma Isadora			60	178
"	6	Schr Watries	Portug'se		86	90

Total number of Chinese arrived.................18,040

Number of Chinese Sailed since May 1, 1852

Date of Sailing	Names of Vessels	Nation	Destinat'n	No of Passengers
May 15	Ship Invincible	American	Hongkong	42
" 26	Ship Courier			3
June 9	Ship Seamen's Bride		Shanghai	1
" 15	Ship Pollock	British	Hongkong	5
July 1	Ship Frederick VII	Danish		20

Total number sailed 71

Number remaining in California 17,969

J Street linking the river from the embarcadero that led to the gold country became the commercial thoroughfare for the mainstream population. The Chinese turned I Street, one block north, into their commercial center. (1855)

PART II

GUM SAAN
YEE FOW

金山二埠

Chinese emigrants aboard the Pacific Mail steamship *Alaska*. May 20, 1876.
(Author's collection)

LANDING OF THE CELESTIALS.---Yesterday evening about five hundred Chinamen who have lately arrived here, landed at Long Wharf with all their baggage. The wharf was covered for a long distance with a perfect forest of basket hats and long tails, rolls of matting and boxes were turned over in all directions, long poles were flourished extensively, and each one appeared to be talking in self defence, making a noise resembling a flock of crows discussing the merits of a cornfield. A large number of persons were collected around, attracted thither by the noise and confusion incidental to the disembarkation of these followers of Confucius. Matters were at last apparently satisfactorily arranged, when each one shouldering a load that would test the strength of a dray horse, started up into the city in single file, to such places as were provided for them by their brethren.

Alta California
August 13, 1852

CHAPTER THREE

Leaving Home

Mass migration of the Chinese from southeast China to foreign lands began well before the California gold rush in 1849. Tens of thousands of laborers had been shipped from the port of Macao to work on the plantations of European colonies. Following the Opium War, Hong Kong became the major port of embarkation. The discovery of gold made California a promising destination for striking it rich—a much better alternative to hard manual labor. The Chinese called California "Gum Saan," or Gold Mountain.

Large scale emigration of the Chinese to California began in 1852. In 1850, there were approximately four thousand Chinese in California. By the year 1852, that number had increased dramatically to twenty thousand.

The Rev. William Dean wrote from Hong Kong on March 29, 1852, "ten or a dozen ships are now about to leave here for San Francisco, each with from two hundred to five hundred passengers."[1] In a span of less than a year, from November 1854 to September 1855, eighteen ships left Hong Kong carrying three thousand Chinese passengers to California.[2] The majority of the travelers were Cantonese from the districts of Sam Yup, Sze Yup, and Heung Shan, all from Guangdong Province.

Anchored in the Hong Kong harbor were scores of British ships and Yankee clippers. The *Galatea*, the *Libertad*, the *Challenge*, the *Stag Hound*, and the *Flying Cloud*—these clippers were America's pride of the sea. Loaded with Chinese cargo for the gold rush population, the ships also were transport for the hundreds of Chinese eagerly awaiting their voyage to Gold Mountain. Gold mania ushered in the California trade for Chinese goods, and launched anew the demand for faster and larger clipper ships.

The thirty to forty days it took to cross the Pacific Ocean was seldom "smooth sailing." The term "su'en fu'ung" (smooth sailing with the wind) came into popular use to bid the emigrant a bon voyage—not only referring to the uncertain and perilous journey faced by the passenger from the unpredictable fury of typhoons, but from avaricious ship owners and their captains. Major abuses and violation of maritime laws were the rule, not the exception. The ships were overloaded with human cargo; people were jammed together in total disregard for health and safety. For example, in July 1854, the *Libertad* left Hong Kong with four hundred passengers on board—one hundred died before they reached San Francisco on July 19, 1854, and after landing, thirty-seven more died.[3]

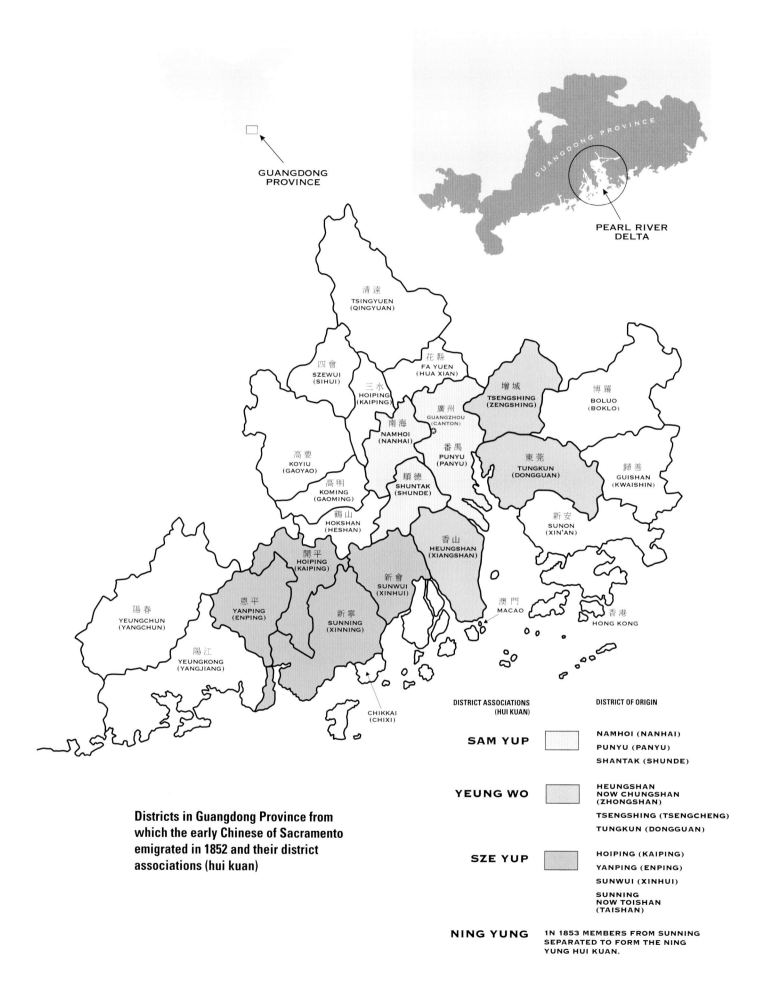

GUANGDONG
PROVINCE

GUANGDONG PROVINCE

PEARL RIVER
DELTA

清遠
TSINGYUEN
(QINGYUAN)

四會
SZEWUI
(SIHUI)

三水
HOIPING
(KAIPING)

花縣
FA YUEN
(HUA XIAN)

增城
TSENGSHING
(ZENGSHING)

博羅
BOLUO
(BOKLO)

高要
KOYIU
(GAOYAO)

廣州
GUANGZHOU
(CANTON)

南海
NAMHOI
(NANHAI)

番禺
PUNYU
(PANYU)

東莞
TUNGKUN
(DONGGUAN)

歸善
GUISHAN
(KWAISHIN)

高明
KOMING
(GAOMING)

順德
SHUNTAK
(SHUNDE)

新安
SUNON
(XIN'AN)

鶴山
HOKSHAN
(HESHAN)

香山
HEUNGSHAN
(XIANGSHAN)

開平
HOIPING
(KAIPING)

恩平
YANPING
(ENPING)

新會
SUNWUI
(XINHUI)

澳門
MACAO

香港
HONG KONG

陽春
YEUNGCHUN
(YANGCHUN)

新寧
SUNNING
(XINNING)

陽江
YEUNGKONG
(YANGJIANG)

CHIKKAI
(CHIXI)

DISTRICT ASSOCIATIONS
(HUI KUAN)

DISTRICT OF ORIGIN

SAM YUP

NAMHOI (NANHAI)

PUNYU (PANYU)

SHANTAK (SHUNDE)

YEUNG WO

HEUNGSHAN
NOW CHUNGSHAN
(ZHONGSHAN)

TSENGSHING (TSENGCHENG)

TUNGKUN (DONGGUAN)

SZE YUP

HOIPING (KAIPING)

YANPING (ENPING)

SUNWUI (XINHUI)

SUNNING
NOW TOISHAN
(TAISHAN)

NING YUNG

1N 1853 MEMBERS FROM SUNNING
SEPARATED TO FORM THE NING
YUNG HUI KUAN.

**Districts in Guangdong Province from
which the early Chinese of Sacramento
emigrated in 1852 and their district
associations (hui kuan)**

CHAPTER FOUR

Yee Fow, The Second City

Upon arrival in San Francisco, newcomers were supported by agents from their own "hui kuan" (district associations based on homeland geographical areas) to assist them. At the district association they were housed, fed, and given medical attention. After a few days, those headed for the northern mines boarded a steamer for the 120-mile trip up the Sacramento River to Sacramento. On board the steamer, a pattern of segregation existed, with the "Oriental" passengers loaded into the "China hold" at the forward end of the hull.[1] Rev. William Taylor reported that his trip to Sacramento aboard the *Senator* took twelve hours. The fare was thirty dollars, a meal was two dollars, and a stateroom for one night was an additional ten dollars.[2]

In November 1849, the *Senator*, the *Mint*, and the *McKim* were the only river boats traveling between San Francisco and Sacramento. By September 1850, there were sixteen steamers in service, and by 1853, when large numbers of Chinese miners were headed to the mines, there were twenty-five.[3] The fare by then had dropped to ten dollars per passenger, and eight dollars per ton of freight.

As in San Francisco, agents from their respective hui kuan welcomed the new arrivals to Sacramento, and escorted them to their headquarters on I Street. These hui kuan were established by and in contact with the San Francisco headquarters. A writer observed, "The human stream of people arrive by boats daily and the streets of Sacramento often present a spectacle of large heavy teams loaded down with broad rim celestials with their neat little Chinese-made rockers bound for the gold mines."[4]

Day and night, teamsters carried hundreds of Chinese from steamship docks to I Street, and transferred tons of freight from the ships onto wagons bound for the Gold Country. The merchants employed about fifty teams making 320 loads per month at forty dollars a load. Twelve to fifteen teams left the city each week for the mines.[5]

Wells Fargo delivered mail to merchants of the Chinese districts through a grocer on the corner of I and Fourth Streets. Chinese merchants sold goods not only to their own community, but to white merchants as well. From his office in the Chinese district, Josiah Gallup operated a thriving business with Chinese merchants of the Yeung Wo and Sze Yup hui kuan.[6] George Elder, another white agent businessman, dealt mainly with the merchants of the Sam Yup hui kuan.[7]

In the hustle and bustle of the gold rush, an immense trade sprang up between Sacramento and the neighboring towns and camps. J Street, linking the river from the embarcadero that led into the Gold Country, became a commercial thoroughfare for the mainstream population. The Chinese turned the adjacent I Street, one block north, into a parallel commercial center for the Chinese.

On March 17, 1852, J. Lamson wrote home giving an account of the gold rush

CHINESE MINERS.

(Author's collection)

While at this camp, I went down the river two or three miles to see a place called Mississippi Bar, where a company of Chinamen were at work . . . There were about a hundred and fifty of them here, living in a perfect village of small tents, all clustered together on the rocks. They had a claim in the bed of the river, which they were working by means of a wing dam . . . The Chinamen's dam was two or three hundred yards in length, and was built of large pine-trees laid one on the top of the other. They must have had great difficulty in handling such immense logs in such a place; but they are exceedingly ingenious in applying mechanical power, particularly in concentrating the force of a large number of men upon one point.

J. D. Borthwick, *Three Years in California,* reprint 1948, p. 215

Chinese mining activities continued into the late 1890s.
(Courtesy of Sacramento Archives and Museum Collection Center)

population. "Among the great number of foreigners in the city the Chinese stand foremost in numbers. They are said to amount to eight hundred to one thousand. Many are encamped on the outskirts of the city. They have many shopkeepers among them..."[8] Likewise, Rev. J. A. Benton, in one of his lectures given before the November 2 fire of 1852, noted that the Chinese occupied almost two blocks comprised of trading and lodging houses, carpenter shops, restaurants, gambling rooms, and a brothel.[9]

While the exact location of the Chinese settlement referenced in Lamson's letter and Benton's lecture is unclear, newspaper reports on a series of fire disasters in Chinatown help place the early beginnings of Chinese settlement in Sacramento. As the *Sacramento Daily Union* reported after the November 2, 1852 fire, the entire Chinese population were seen moving onto I Street above Fifth, "from K Street between Fifth and Sixth."

Not long after they had settled down in their new locations, a second disastrous fire swept the area on July 13, 1854 on Fifth Street between I and J Streets. The Chinese lost no time rebuilding, but one year later on July 3, 1855, a fire started in the Sze Yup building, and again burned the quarters on the north side of I Street.

The 1850 U.S. Census recorded 9,087 persons, with only six Chinese in Sacramento. Their names and occupations, as nearly as can be deciphered, are three miners, Tun Chun (age twenty), John Wun (age fifteen), Osin Wun (age twenty-five), and a cook named Ouni (age twenty-five), and listed under "Canton House," Comsun (age thirty-eight) and John Besinti Yongne (age thirty).

The 1851 Sacramento City Directory and the 1853-1854 directory did not list any Chinese participants in the gold rush society. Yet a county census taken in 1852 footnoted the presence of 804 Chinese men and eight Chinese women in Sacramento, within a total population of 6,820.

Census takers were notorious for inaccurate reporting, caused by carelessness, language barriers, and illegible handwriting. The proper names were recorded with the prefix "Ah" followed by a name, which could be a given name or a surname. "Ah" itself was not part of a name but part of a speech pattern. Unfortunately, the 1860 U.S. Census listed 929 Chinese as "Ah" followed by a single syllable name. The difficulty in identifying early Chinese immigrants is further compounded by the fact that there wasn't a standardized romanization. The spelling depended on the ingenuity and skill of the individual census taker. In addition, because of the many dialect differences, the same proper name and surname are pronounced differently, and therefore phonetically recorded differently.

The record of deaths for the City of Sacramento is no more reliable than the census. The first recorded death of a Chinese person on September 25, 1851, refers merely to a "Chinaman." A subsequent listing in the year 1860 refers to the deceased as "Ah" plus a name with their district origin.

Detailed accounts of the lives of the earliest Sacramento Chinese are forever lost. Only by gathering information from contemporary observers, writers, and official records are we able to piece together a minimal mosaic of the Chinese presence in Sacramento. These pioneers nevertheless laid the foundation that was the beginning of the Chinese community in Sacramento.

(Author's collection)

YEE FUNG CHUNG, PIONEER

Oral tradition has it that Yee Fung Chung arrived in Sacramento during the gold rush and subsequently went on to Fiddletown where he established the Chew Kee store and began his herbal practice. Another tradition places him back in Sacramento during Governor Leland Stanford's administration. The Governor's wife, Jane, was not well and doctors were not able to diagnose her illness. One evening Mrs. Stanford was in severe discomfort and the Chinese cook suggested calling Yee Fung Chung, the herbalist. Fung Chung was called to the mansion to treat Mrs. Stanford and she "miraculously" recovered after drinking the herbal medicine brewed by Fung Chung.

Fung Chung also set up practice in Virginia City with his son Yee Lok Sam and Yee Toy on October 3, 1869, at which time he used his second birth name "Wah Hing." In the recorder's office in Storey County is a document in Chinese filed by Wah Hing on September 24, 1886,[10] certifying it as a medical diploma issued in Hong Kong. F. A. Bee, consul for the Chinese consulate in San Francisco, also filed a translation of the document in December 1886.

An incident occurred when Wah Hing set up his practice among the Chinese population in Virginia City.[11] His reputation of healing prowess quickly spread throughout the community at large to the dismay of three young Caucasian doctors. The trio found Wah Hing's curative effectiveness too competitive, and challenged his qualifications. They demanded proof of his right to practice medicine. In response, Wah Hing requested documents from Hong Kong. When a copy of his alleged medical diploma arrived, it came complete with diagrams identifying acupoints of the body where pressure was to be applied to stimulate and correct imbalances of the body's internal organs. The document was displayed and presented to the public along with Consul Bee's translation. The diploma was actually a testimonial letter to Wah Hing's medical studies and qualifications with the signatures of six well known herb doctors in Hong Kong. Since no Caucasian (at the time) could read Chinese, Consul Bee's translation was accepted, and Wah Hing's qualification was undisputed. The three doctors quietly retreated.

Wah Hing was back in Sacramento during the years 1901 to 1906. In 1901, he advertised his practice in the *Evening Bee* at 1209 Third Street. In 1905, he filed a partnership with the Immigration Service using his surname "Yee" Wah Hing, doing business at 725 J Street. His son Yee Lok Sam appeared on the same list as T. Wah Hing. Also on that list were the sons of T. Wah Hing, Willie and Philip, and the following unidentified Hings: Hong, Tuck, Toy, Mow, Woy, and Sue.

For reasons unknown, Yee Lok Sam adopted the use of his father's name Wah Hing in about 1894 and added "T" to the name at about 1897. He assumed the name Yee Lok Sam in about 1910 and continued to use that name at 725 J Street until retirement.

1857 view of Sutter Lake. The lake became popularly known as China Slough because of the Chinese settlement on I Street between Second and Fifth Streets. The north side of I Street is submerged at this section and the Third Street plank walk had not yet been built.

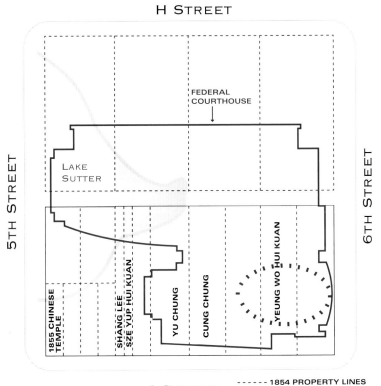

The present site of the Federal Courthouse on the block bounded by H and I Streets, and Fifth and Sixth Streets, was where the Chinese settlement existed in 1852. (Courtesy of Brian W. Choy)

Even in the frantic pace of the gold rush, there was time for entertainment and recreation. In mid-1852, a huge placard posted outside the community announced performances were to be given by Chinese magicians and jugglers.[12] On February 17, 1855, the *Sacramento Daily Union* reported a puppet theatre was opened near Fifth Street during New Year. These performances were not only for the Chinese but were devised for the general public. A reporter wrote, "Non-Chinese, including senators and assemblymen, sat in the audience...much of the acting was of superior quality." On March 28, 1859, the Chinese celebrated the Dragon Boat Festival, racing their colorful dragon boats on Sutter Lake to the delight of spectators who termed it "striking and exciting."

On a more somber note, the Chinese joined the city in mourning the lives lost on January 27, 1855, when the steamer *Pearl* exploded on the river while returning from Marysville. Steamboat explosions were a common occurrence as captains raced each other and recklessly fed the boilers to make time. Fifty-six persons were killed on the *Pearl*, among them a large number of Chinese. The city officials set apart a day for a funeral procession. Over three thousand people gathered to observe the proceedings. Some were mourners, others were curious onlookers attracted by the Chinese procession headed by priests and musicians. Burning candles, exploding firecrackers, and gold leaf paper filled the air.[13]

For a brief period the Sacramento Chinese community was able to support a newspaper. Ze Too Yune (Henry Tsai) published the *Chinese Daily News* at the southwest corner of Third and I Streets from December 1856 through 1857. It sold for twenty-five cents per week and had a circulation of two hundred. The only surviving copy of an issue of that newspaper carries news not only from Hong Kong but also from Marysville and noted the results of a recent Sacramento election. As this paper demonstrates, it is a misconception that the Chinese kept to themselves and made no effort to assimilate—the Chinese actually kept abreast of current events. Henry Tsai subsequently established a school for Chinese children where both the Chinese and English languages were taught.[14]

The discovery of gold placed California in a strategic position for America's evangelical movement, the Second Great Awakening. With California fronting Asia, religious leaders enthusiastically recognized its potential. For years, missionaries had traveled to China, and now they found thousands of Chinese in California who might carry the gospel back to their own people in China. For the missionaries, the gold was not in the gold fields, but in the potential to convert thousands of Chinese in California.

As written by Rev. William Taylor, "God in his providence has forty thousand long-queue fellows in California, at no expense to anybody, studying the English language, through which the gospel message will reach their hearts, and then, they, by the thousand, it may be, can return on the principle we have illustrated, and carry the tidings of salvation to the perishing millions of their own land."[15]

The first Chinese chapel was built on the northeast corner of Sixth and H Streets. It was dedicated on June 10, 1855, by Rev. John Lewis Shuck, who delivered the first Chinese sermon in Sacramento, followed by a sermon

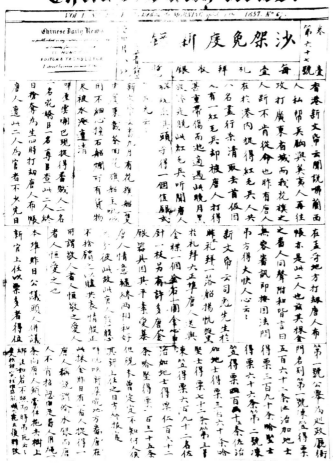

Chinese Baily News.

Chinese Baily News.

VOL. 1, WEDNESDAY MORNING, APRIL 8TH, 1857, ISSUE #67

In Marysville and Yuba City, two robbers, Ferguson and Johnson were arrested. These two men made their living on robbery. Chinese camps were victimized by them many times.	Newspaper - In September a ship came here from China with a load of tea. Captain Lindsey, an American, whose ship hit a rock, damaged the ship and all the cargoes were soaked wet.	Hong Kong Newspaper - The French people secretly helped the British subjects with money and military equipment to attack Canton again. But the U.S. people would not take the order to join them. Yesterday the Chinese peoples arrested eight red haired 'British' soldiers, then chopped their heads off after killing them. Another red haired solder was injured seriously but escaped, because the night was dark. According to the Chinese, for each head they chop off, they will get the reward of $200.00.
Local News - Town Hall meeting yesterday to elect sheriff for this town. The primary voting results show. *1st precinct:* Dunlap-562 Carney-390 Hopkins-66 *2nd precinct:* Dunlap-425 Carney-360 Hopkins-72	Mr. Spiel set sail to return home this Monday. Two days before the departure, Chinese people in San Francisco gave him a farewell gift including a gold watch, a gold nugget, a golden necktie clip and several pieces of Chinese gold and silver. All these years he has respected the Chinese people for their true friendship and without prejudice they get along very well. To show their appreciation, the Chinese people earnestly bestowed him such beautiful gifts. As the Chinese proverb says, "If one respects and loves another person, one will return the same."	A few days ago, these two men broke the law again in Mumford. All the gold miners said, to satisfy the public, they should be hung without a trial.
Marysville and Sonora - Americans and Chinese were working in the gold mine when an American accused a Chinese person of stealing Mercury. The Chinese person denied the charge. Then the accuser put a rope around his neck, tied him up on a tree, threatening him with death by hanging him. The Chinese person said that was a real grievance. He'd rather die than admit a crime that he never committed. Finally, he was released.	*3rd precinct:* Dunlap-692, Carney-562, Hopkins-135. At present time, we do not know who is the winner. Have to wait until the total votes are counted on the inaugural day.	

(Courtesy of Chinese American Council of Sacramento

The first Chinese chapel erected on the northeast corner of Sixth and H Streets was founded by Rev. John Lewis Shuck of the Baptist Church on June 10, 1855. (Courtesy of Sacramento Archives and Museum Center Collection)

REVEREND SHUCK

Rev. Shuck, the first Baptist minister to set foot in China, arrived with his eighteen-year-old bride, Henrietta Hall, in 1835. For eight years he served in Hong Kong and Canton until Henrietta died, leaving four young children. Rev. Shuck decided to return home. In 1847 he returned to China with a second Mrs. Shuck, this time serving in Shanghai. The second Mrs. Shuck also died and Rev. Shuck again returned home to Charleston, South Carolina. In April 1854 he was called to Sacramento where he stayed in the community until 1860 when he returned home.

by Ah Mooey, the first Chinese baptized in Sacramento. Some two hundred persons attended the service with standing room only. Half were American ladies and gentlemen, the other half were Chinese. The Board of Southern Baptist Convention sent Rev. Shuck to Sacramento in April 1854, where he served as minister to the First Baptist Church and as missionary to the Chinese of the city. While Rev. Shuck was quick to establish the Chinese Baptist Mission in 1855, other denominations followed somewhat later.

CHINA SLOUGH AND TONG YUN GAI

In the 1860s, the city blocks between H and I Streets and Fifth and Sixth Streets were increasingly used for warehousing. The Chinese had by then expanded westward on I Street, between Second and Fifth Streets. Because portions of the parcels on the north side of I Street formed the south shore of Sutter Lake, the lake became popularly known as China Slough. The Chinese called I Street "Tong Yun Gai" (the street of the Chinese).[16] The Central Pacific Railroad occupied the land across the lake on the north side, and the 1895 Sanborn map shows railroad spurs running right down the center of I Street. As an unsavory aside, the railroad, the Chinese, and the citizens of the city used the lake as a dumping place for their refuse, creating a gigantic cesspool.

The *Sacramento Daily Union* on January 11, 1873, described the daily activities of the Chinese, "You will find them in the mines, on the farms, on their own vegetable patches, in wash houses, in every factory, in fact, at every point where industry is at work."

By dawn, the district came to life. Farmers from Slaters Addition and gardens lying between R Street levee and Sutterville trucked their vegetables to the intersection of J and Third Streets, where vendors jostled each other with their poles and baskets, and congregated to select produce to be sold throughout the city. These vegetable vendors traveled a great deal on foot each day. Before daylight, merchants laid out their products of pastries, fruit, and an unending variety of other foodstuffs. While not unlike the food we see in today's Chinese markets, the food was looked upon as strange and suspicious by the white population, few of whom had ever seen or tasted Chinese food. Barbecue pork glazed with honey (cha-siu) or perhaps a roasted pig with its skin fired to a golden brown, was described dubiously by one writer as "varnished pork." Live ducks and chickens stuffed into bamboo cages quacked and clucked incessantly while fish floundered in water bins and awaited their fates. Itinerant cobblers and carpenters set out tools of their trade and arranged their benches ready for the day's work.

The back of the I Street dwellings overhung the south shore of Sutter Lake and Chinese laundrymen washed clothing from floating platforms tethered at the shoreline. The laundry guild, through which the Chinese regulated their tradesmen throughout the city, was located on I Street between Fourth and Fifth Streets. Its registry listed fifty-five laundries and three hundred laundrymen on I Street.

Two shoe and slipper manufacturers, one on Third Street between J and K Streets, and the other on K Street between Third and Fourth Streets, virtually monopolized the footwear business. Among the many other

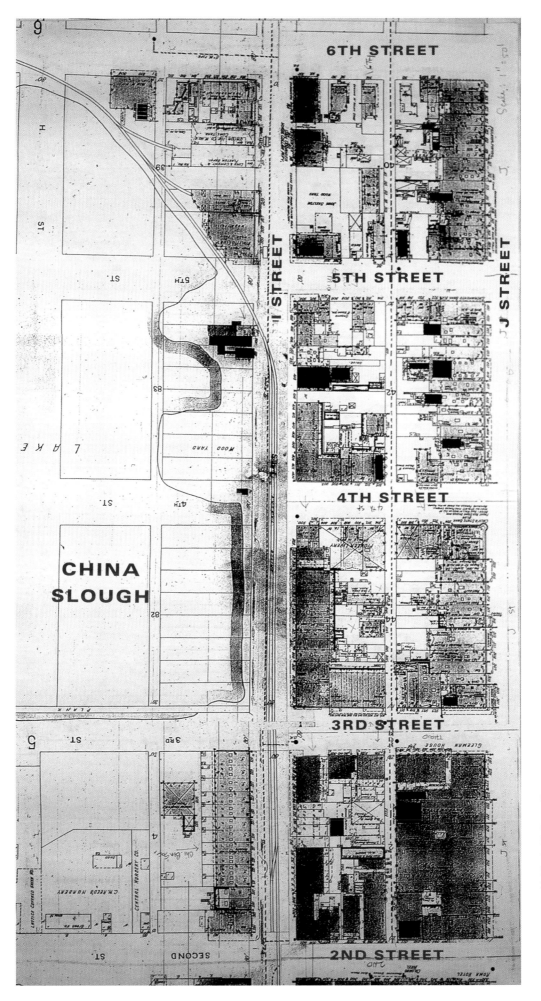

1895 Sanborn fire insurance map.

Chinese tenement housing and businesses were on I Street between 2nd and 5th Streets.

This 1873 scene of the Chinese quarters along the southern shore of China Slough depicts the submerged rear of the I Street properties. To increase usable space, wooden shacks were extended over the water, supported by woodpiles. To discourage this practice, an 1870 city ordinance prohibited the occupancy or the use of any building extended over water. (Author's collection)

APPLETONS' JOURNAL.

No. 203] NEW YORK, AUGUST 30, 1873. [Vol. X.

CHINESE QUARTERS, SACRAMENTO

Laundrymen on south shore of China Slough. Height of piles is exaggerated. (Author's collection)

Third Street plank walk over China Slough. (Courtesy of Sacramento Archives and Museum Collection Center)

The Chinese built floating laundry work stations on platforms tethered to the shoreline at the rear of the I Street properties. Each platform accommodated one man with his table, tubs, and baskets. (Author's collection)

Domestic servants on their day off. (Author's collection)

stores were twenty-five cigar makers, a pawnshop, three eatery houses, six lotteries, and six herb shops. Seven herb doctors and twelve barbers provided service for some six hundred residents of the Chinese quarters. There were three interpreters: Ah Sing, known as "Charlie," worked in the police court; Ah Hing was an agent for the railroad company; and Ah Bean worked for the Wah Hing wholesale market. Wells Fargo did a thriving business providing financial and express services to ninety-six businesses in the Chinese quarter.

Two slaughter yards located outside the city limits, owned and operated by Chinese, slaughtered numerous hogs daily, not only for Chinese markets but for white butcher shops as well. Chinese meat markets were identified in Chinese as "pork" shops, probably indicating that the meat consumption of the Chinese consisted mainly of pork. Two of the Chinese butcher shops, Wah Kee and Wah Sing, were on I Street between Second and Third. The owner of one of these shops was Ah You, who had been in California for sixteen years since 1860 and had been in Sacramento since 1863.

To an extent, the Chinese were tolerated outside the Chinese quarters as long as they worked in the service industries in saloons and hotels, and as cooks, houseboys, and gardeners in affluent homes.

Evenings on I Street were no less lively than the days—only the sounds differentiated the night from the hustle and bustle of the daytime commerce. The not so euphonious clashing of cymbals and syncopated rhythmic drumming on wood blocks from the orchestra in the theatre, reverberated into the night and signaled the beginning of the first act of the Cantonese opera.

Inside the gambling houses, the croupier tossed a handful of "chin" (Chinese copper and brass coins) onto the gaming table of fantan. Gamblers placed their bets, unconcerned with the commotion of the Chinese Christians marching outside with torches and singing hymns led by Rev. D. D. Jones and Chin Toy from the M. E. Mission. Nevertheless, Chin Toy, a loyal convert, undauntedly boasted, "we wake them up."[17]

When the vegetable vendors returned exhausted from hawking their produce throughout the city, they would anxiously drop their empty baskets and rush to check the results of their "bok gop bew" (Chinese lottery tickets). For those not working in the gold fields, playing the lottery gave them hope of striking it rich.

Those eager to learn the English language retreated to one of the churches where classes were conducted. A. Sherman held a class in the basement at the Congregational Church on I Street between Sixth and Seventh and charged a small fee to defray expenses. Andrew Aitkin conducted an English class at the Presbyterian Church on Sixth and L Streets. The Presbyterian Church also had a Chinese Mission School on Fourth Street between J and I Streets and the Methodist Church held evening English classes on the corner of Fifth and I Streets. The eagerness of the Chinese to learn English demonstrated that the Chinese recognized early on the importance of being able to communicate outside the confines of Chinese society.

While the churches hoped to win Chinese to the gospel with the attraction of conducting English classes, proceedings of the State Commission on the growing evil of Chinese immigration took testimony on the subject as to whether a Chinese could be converted to Christianity or not.

(Author's collection)

Evenings on I Street were no less lively than days. Inside the gambling houses, the coupier tossed a handful of "Chin" onto the "table of fantan." For those not working in the gold fields, playing the lottery gave them hope of striking it rich.

KENO

The lottery game known as keno, which is played in today's casinos in Reno and Las Vegas, is a direct copy of the Chinese lottery called "bok gop bew" (white pigeon ticket) that was played in Chinese communities for over one hundred years until its operation was shut down by authorities shortly after World War II. The original Chinese version consisted of eighty characters taken from the first eighty characters of the "One Thousand Word Classics." The keno version is simplified by using the numbers one through eighty.

Lotteries appeared as early as the 1860s in Sacramento. Ah Cow, a merchant, won a lottery and the house refused to pay so he snitched on the gambling house by reporting to the authorities of its operation. Shortly thereafter he was found dead.

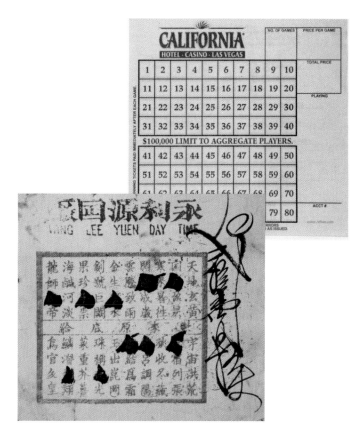

SENATE TESTIMONY

From the testimony before the Senate Committee, Charles Jones, District Attorney, talked about tribunal records confiscated from a room on I Street between Fourth and Fifth, as follows:

There was a Chinaman here who opened a wash-house on Second Street, underneath the Orleans Hotel. It appears that he was a member of the Chinese Wash-house Association, and that they had a rule that no wash-house should be opened within ten doors of one already opened. The new house was opened within the prescribed limits, and the Association held a meeting. One of the charges was that he was in partnership with a white man—a foreigner, their rules forbidding any such arrangement, and they fined him, I think, thirty dollars. The Chinaman went to Mr. Fratt, who told him he would protect him. Then they held another meeting, and, as was proved on the trial of these cases, they determined that he should pay one hundred and ten dollars, or they would kill him. They sent out three of their number, and they met him on Third, between I and J... He had sixty dollars in his pocket, and he gave them that. He went and told Mr. Fratt, and these three men were arrested for robbery... (The records were taken and translated for the trial of the robbery case.)

According to the records confiscated from the wash-house association, members enter into a solemn compact to abide by the rules of the association, including that no wash-house be opened within ten doors of one already opened, and that no member enter into partnership with a foreigner. The association had its own fines and penalties, ultimately including death, and moreover a structured system for compensating the contract killer, including counsel to defend him, compensation for jail time, and money sent home to his relatives should he die. The wash-house records appeared in evidence and were admitted as was a poster offering a reward for the killing of this man...

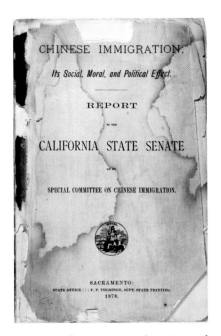

Testimony from witnesses here-in are from the 1876 report on the investigation of the Chinese population held in Sacramento and San Francisco on the evils of immigration.

Testimony of Lem Schaum, who came from China when he was fifteen and was educated in Oakland by Mr. Rowle, Rev. Moore, and Dr. Gample, when asked about Christianity among the Chinese:

Q: Have you tried to make Christians out of your countrymen here?

A: I tried that; but it is very hard work to do it.

Q: Do some of them pretend to be Christians when they are not?

A: Only those grown up fellows; the young boys do not. Boys working around see the American customs, and we can instruct them in no time; but the old ones think Confucius is the only good religion, and with them it is very hard work.

When asked how many Christian Chinese there were in Sacramento, he answered, "I guess about twenty-four."

BILLY HO LUNG

Billy Ho Lung worked in a saloon and for the Pony Exchange. He attempted mining in 1848 but settled in Sacramento in 1862. In 1876 he became a labor contractor located on 66 I Street, corner of Third Street. Billy was among those who was subpoenaed to give testimony during the 1876 investigation of the Chinese population conducted by the state on the "monstrous evil and curse" upon the citizens of California.

One focus of the investigation was to document that all Chinese women in California were prostitutes. Another focus was to document that the presence of the Chinese was leading to the degradation of society by taking jobs that otherwise would go to young women. A large focus of the investigation was the extent to which Chinese could or could not be converted to Christianity.

Billy was interrogated thusly:

Q. Six years ago, when you were with the Pony Exchange, did you not buy a woman and give six hundred dollars for her? A. Yes sir, I bought me a wife.

Q. Where in San Francisco is she living? A. On Jackson Street.

Q. How many women are with her? A. She is alone.

Q. How many times do you see your wife? A. Sometime.

Q. Are you married to her? A. Yes, Sir.

Q. Why don't you keep her in Sacramento? A. She quarrels with me.

Testimony of Sam Lee:

Q: Do you know any Christian Chinamen?

A: No, sir. I went to school once to learn something. I wanted to learn to speak English, and the American law.

There was substantial agreement among all testifying that the Chinese did not convert to Christianity so much as they wanted to learn the language. On the other hand, testimony by Andrew Aitkin gave evidence that some Chinese had indeed become Christians.

Q: What knowledge have you as to the efforts that have been made on this coast by the Christian people to convert and bring to Christianity the Chinese people?

A: My knowledge, as far as I have assisted and observed the labors of others, is that it is beneficial.

Q: What is beneficial—what has been done?

A: Teaching them to read the English language, studying scripture, and quite a number have been converted to Christianity. There have been nine of them made members of the Presbyterian Church; of that number, one has died.

Q: For what length of time have you observed these matters?

A: I have been giving my personal attention for about three years—two years and a half or three years. I have been Superintendent of the Chinese School in the Presbyterian Church. That school is on the corner of Sixth and L Streets, and is under the management of the Presbyterian Session.

Q: What is the employment of these persons that belong to your church?

A: Some are engaged in washing, and some are servants.

Q: Do you know how they are received by the Chinese who are not Christians?

A. They are persecuted a good deal. I will state that a boy living with Judge Curtis, and who died a year ago, was as good a Christian as ever lived in the world. He was the first Chinese member of our church.

That boy was none other than Ye Gon Lun.[18] He came to work in the household of Judge N. Greene Curtis in 1865 at the age of nine. When he was fifteen years old, he was drawn to the gospel, inspired by a sermon given by the Rev. Ira Condit. He was later baptized and expressed the desire to preach to his own countrymen. However, he became ill and another Chinese boy named Lee Yin came to take over the household duties. Ye Gon Lun never recovered and died at the age of eighteen in 1874. Judge Curtis marked his grave with an eight-foot tall monument. Lee Yin served the Curtis household for awhile, but returned home to China to preach the gospel. His wife hated the unfamiliar religion and in despair attempted suicide. Upon failing, she took a rope and tried to strangle her husband while he was asleep. Ultimately, she accepted Christianity.

Rapid development of mining, railroads, and agriculture made Sacramento the second most important city in the state and by 1882, the Chinese called it "Yee Fow" (Second City).[19] Yee Fow likewise continued to be the major supply center for Chinese miners in the mother lode, and to the Chinese throughout the Sacramento valley. These industries created opportunities for the Chinese in Sacramento, and their population flourished. By the same token, Chinese laborers stimulated the growth of industry in California. The Chinese population in the city rose from 600 to its peak of 1,781 in 1880.

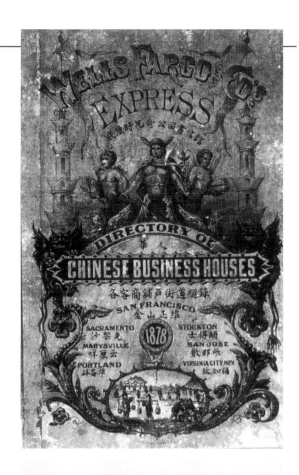

The 1878 Wells Fargo Chinese Directory references I Street as Tong Yun Gai. (Courtesy Wells Fargo History Room)

I Street, known to the Chinese as Tong Yun Gai (Chinese Street), circa 1880.
(Courtesy of Sacramento Archives and Museum Collection Center)

PROLOGUE

Even before the discussion of large scale immigration of Chinese occurred, debate was raging over whether California should be a slave state or become a free state populated by free white men. During the framing of the first constitution of California, delegates focused the debate in racial terms of white superiority over the inferiority of the "Negro" race. The fear and anxiety over the perceived evils of slave masters working their slaves in the mines and of free blacks competing with white labor compelled California's first lawmakers to declare "neither slavery nor involuntary servitude shall be tolerated" in this state. These debates proved moot with the increasing rate of Chinese immigration.

In 1850, African Americans in California numbered about one thousand, and the Chinese numbered six hundred sixty. By 1852, the Chinese numbered over twenty thousand. California's "colored" population was Chinese, and the perceived fear of labor competition was no longer from African Americans. For the next fifty years, California was obsessed with ridding the state of the Chinese. The elimination of the Chinese began in the mines and later spread to the industrial, commercial, and agricultural development of the state. As the frontier developed, the Chinese were recruited as the primary source of labor, but as Chinese labor came into competition with white labor, conflict inevitably arose. Expressed in racial terms of white superiority over yellow inferiority, the conflict became nationally known as the "Chinese Question." The answer was the passage of the Exclusion Act of May 1882, an attempt to eliminate the presence of the Chinese. Sinophobia and anti-Chinese hysterics continued unabated for the next two decades. Yet it was still the availability of Chinese labor which helped develop California's economy in such a remarkably short time.

Governor George Perkins declared the fourth day of March, 1882 a legal holiday for anti-Chinese demonstrations.

(Author's collection)

NIGHTMARE IN THE AMERICAN DREAM

美夢破碎

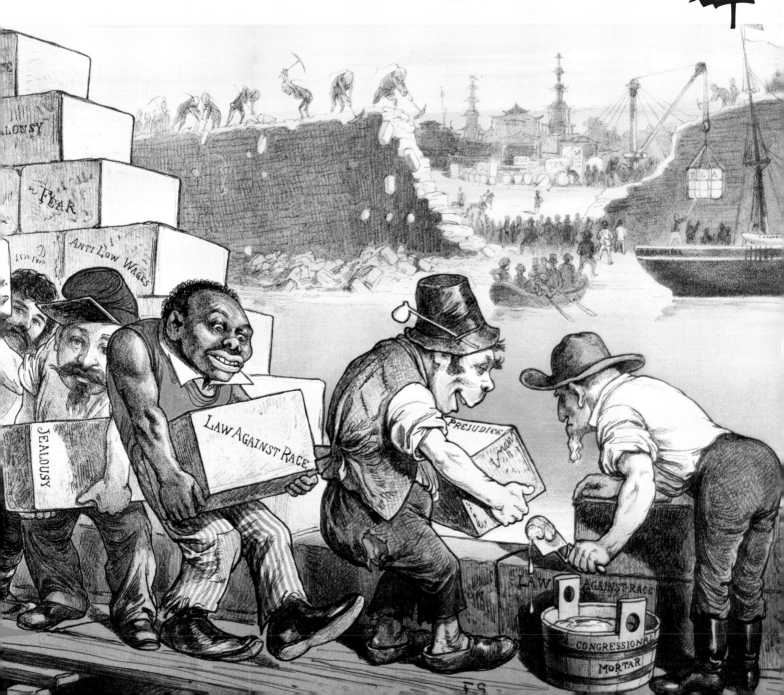

Using only hand shovels, wheelbarrows, and horse-drawn scrappers, thousands of Chinese reclaimed the swampland along the Sacramento River from Sherman Island to the city of Sacramento. The reclaimed land was in turn leased to Chinese sharecroppers. By the 1870s, agricultural labor was predominantly Chinese.

CHINAMEN ON TULE LANDS.

A letter from Emmaton states that the farmers are busy planting potatoes on the tule islands. The Chinamen are meeting with great success in their cultivation of tule lands. They appear to thoroughly understand the cultivation of these reclaimed swamps. They lease a tract at a good price, for cash, then they club together, plough and plant, and soon secure large returns for their labor. Quite a number have leased land at Emmaton at $15 per acre, and are now busy in every direction.

DAC April 2, 1871

CHAPTER FIVE

Moving Earth and Mountain

The 1945 Sacramento City Directory cites: "Historically Sacramento is associated with three epochal events in California's development. The settlement established August 12, 1830, by Capt. John A. Sutter . . . marked the beginning of agricultural development that has made California the third among the states of the Union in total value of its agricultural products. The discovery of gold January 24, 1848, by James W. Marshall . . . The transcontinental railroad . . . first to link the west to the east and from the viewpoint of lasting benefits overshadows even Marshall's discovery . . . "

These lasting benefits were in no small way contributed to by the availability of Chinese cheap labor. The mass emigration of Chinese triggered by the deterioration of the Manchu empire was coincident with the development of America's western frontier. During the early years of gold mania the potential agricultural greatness of the state had yet to begin. Transportation from west to east was still by ships sailing ninety days by way of Cape Horn.

With the help of the Chinese, swampland was reclaimed to become productive farmland, which was in turn leased back to Chinese tenant farmers for crops harvested by Chinese workers. With the completion of the transcontinental railroad, using some twelve thousand Chinese laborers, transportation made possible the shipping of perishable crops. With this increased cultivation of crops, the canning industry developed, again predominately manned by Chinese laborers.

In the employment of the thousands of workers, a contract labor system evolved. A middleman called the labor contractor, became essential to the recruiting of laborers. With the workers not speaking English, and the employer not speaking Chinese, a Chinese person with a rudimentary knowledge of English became crucial for negotiating conditions of a contract.

The system worked to the advantage of the employer as the conditions of the contract were negotiated directly with the labor contractor, who agreed to supply a specified number of laborers at a given time to perform a prescribed job for a set sum of money. The employer paid the labor contractor directly, and therefore, the tedious responsibility of hiring, timekeeping, and bookkeeping for individual payroll was not necessary. Furthermore, the lodging and board, the maintenance of campsites, and the supervision of the workers, was the responsibility of the labor contractor. The labor contractor, generally a merchant, supplied provisions for the workers and distributed the payroll after deducting the expenses. The owner was responsible only to supply the tools necessary for the job to be done. When the work was done, the laborers picked up their possessions and moved on to the next job.

"We had a very large wheat field. It was harvest time . . . the superintendent (sent for) a couple of hundred of white men . . . those men would not work more than two to three days a week, and they would quit . . . I then went to a Chinaman and told him I wanted to contract for binding and shocking wheat . . . several hundred came. We had one or two hundred acres that needed putting up very badly; and the next morning, it was all in shock. The Chinamen did the work that night. They did the work well . . . and we abandoned white labor."[1]

The Chinese were the predominate race comprising migratory labor by 1870, until the passage of the Exclusion Act of 1882. California's migratory labor history began with the Chinese using the contract labor system and that system persisted with the Japanese, Filipinos, and Hispanics who followed. Even with the success of Caesar Chavez's unionized United Farm Workers, the problems of California's agricultural labor persist to this day.

RECLAMATION AND AGRICULTURE

Within the Sacramento and San Joaquin River Deltas lay five hundred thousand acres of tule swampland, nothing but muck and mosquito-infested decaying grass. When reclaimed, this land could be transformed into productive agricultural land. The federal Swampland Act, passed in 1850, made it possible to purchase government land in California for about a dollar an acre, with certain contingencies. When 50 percent or more of the swampland was reclaimed, the land would be deeded to the persons who had reclaimed the swampland.

The Chinese were called upon to undertake this difficult task of reclamation. As said by Governor John McDougal, ". . . our newly-adopted citizens, the Chinese, could

be well utilized as they are particularly suited to the climate and character of these lands." Senator George Tingley shared the sentiments of the governor, and introduced a bill in March 1852, for the importation of Chinese contract laborers. Even subsequent Governor John Bigler, who sounded the first anti-Chinese alarm against Chinese immigration, had no objection to Asiatic labor, as long as they were confined to draining the swampland.[2]

Building levees and ditches required manual labor using only shovels, wheel barrels, and horses. Oftentimes men worked waist deep in water. The number of Chinese working on a single project sometimes reached three or four thousand. The average levee was 140 feet wide at the bottom, 30 feet wide at the top, and 16 feet high.

Governor McDougal's prediction that the Chinese "if well utilized . . . would make swamps productive and contribute largely to the State Treasury" became reality. After reclamation, the price of land soared from a few dollars to more than one hundred dollars an acre. The demand for land also soared, and corporations bought up land along with the few individuals who saw the potential. The Tide Land Reclamation Company acquired 250,000 acres within a few years. Another speculator took up a tract of land embracing four townships.[3] The large tracts of land led to large scale farming, which in turn, demanded intense seasonal labor.

The introduction of clamshell dredgers in 1876 made the Chinese laborers obsolete in swamp reclamation. Instead, they went into farming and worked as farm laborers. Grand Island, Brannan Island, and Sherman Island were reclaimed by the Chinese and leased back to the Chinese for tenant farming. Sherman Island alone had fourteen thousand acres devoted to growing grapes, strawberries, watermelons, and muskmelons. From the 1870s until the passage of the Exclusion Act of 1882, Chinese farms and laborers predominated. By 1910, the Portuguese, Italians, and Japanese outnumbered the Chinese.

THE RAILROADS

As early as 1815, Congress had discussed the building of a railroad to bridge the continent, a major purpose of which was to facilitate trade with China. In 1861, the Central Pacific Railroad of California was incorporated. The principals, Leland Stanford, Charles Crocker, Collis P. Huntington, and Mark Hopkins, were known as the "Big Four." The Central Pacific broke ground in Sacramento on January 8, 1863, and began building eastward towards the Sierra Nevada mountain range. After two years, only thirty-one miles of track had been laid. Lack of capital and a shortage of labor brought the work to a stop at Newcastle. Looming before them and above their heads were the tall peaks of the Sierra Nevada. Once out of the foothills, the roadbed had to be carved into the cliff at Cape Horn, 1,400 feet above the American River. Thirteen tunnels over one thousand feet long had to be drilled through solid granite.

When Leland Stanford spoke against the immigration of the Chinese, little did he realize that those same "dregs" of Asia would be called upon as the solution to the labor problems of the Big Four. Charles Crocker suggested employing the Chinese over the objection of Chief Construction Superintendent J. H. Strobridge. The first fifty Chinese hired proved highly successful and more were hired. By May 1866, the Central

Sacramento Bee, Oct. 11, 1859. (Courtesy of Wendell W. Huffman).

Pacific had reached Secrettown, sixty-two miles from Sacramento. Progress had bogged down again. The local supply of Chinese laborers was insufficient. The Central Pacific then recruited thousands more from China. They were young men from the rural districts of Sunning (now Toishan) and Sunhui in Guangdong Province.[4] By 1869, an army of twelve thousand Chinese had stormed over the Sierra mountains on the way to Promontory Point in Utah, moving earth and mountain as they went. For example, it took one year to blast and bore through 1,659 feet of rock to create Summit Tunnel Number 6, which was placed seven thousand feet above Donner Lake.

Using hand labor and one-horse carts, ten thousand Chinese "moved mountains" in the construction of the railroad. (Courtesy of Southern Pacific)

(Author's collection)

Eighty-three individuals and stores supplied provisions and/or acted as gang bosses or labor contractors for Chinese laborers. Hung Wah Company was consistently the most active.

The Chinese railroad laborers worked under a gang boss who distributed their wages of $1.25 per day, from which he deducted food and other living expenses. White laborers were paid $1.15 per day but with board included.

According to railroad payroll records, in January 1864, Hung Wah Company received $699.12 for 587.5 days of work at $1.19 per day for twenty-two laborers. Ah Toy, "Chinese foreman," received $23.28 for 24.25 days at $0.96 per day while a white foreman, M. G. Shiplar, received $2.50 per day.[5] This belies the often repeated story by historians that Crocker persuaded Strobridge to use Chinese laborers as an experiment for the first time in the spring of 1865. Even before the Central Pacific Railroad broke ground, some 250 Chinese had worked on the San Francisco and Marysville railroad, as reported by The Sacramento Bee on October 11, 1859. The railroad became the California Pacific.

The Central Pacific Railroad won a celebrated race against the Union Pacific Railroad for laying the most track in one day. The eight names of the Irish track layers for the Central Pacific were memorialized on the time sheet: George Elliot, Edward Kelleen, Thomas Daley, Mike Shaw, Mike Sullivan, Mike Kenedy, Fred McNamare, and Patrick Joice.[6] The names of the Chinese crew responsible for laying the ties as part of the team were not.

The number of Chinese lives lost building the transcontinental railroad is unknown to this day, and their sacrifices in large part unheralded. At the summit tunnel in the Sierra Nevada, nitroglycerine was used for the first time in lieu of black powder. The unstable chemical often exploded prematurely, killing scores of Chinese workers. The Chinese labored under the scorching sun of summer and the howling blizzards of winter. During the severe winter of 1866–1867, avalanches swept camps and crews down the slope. In the spring, frozen bodies were found with picks or shovels still clutched in their hands. The Sacramento Reporter on June 30, 1870, noted a train coming from the Sierra Nevada with twenty thousand pounds of accumulated bones. It was estimated to be the remains of about 1,200 Chinese who died working on the railroad. The boys from Sunning and Sunhui were finally going home.

The completion of the first transcontinental railroad marked the beginning of an epoch of railroad building throughout the west. Many of the Chinese, now experienced railroad workers, continued to work on the railroads. A few retired in Utah after a lifetime of service. Others returned to Sacramento to work in the railroad shops or to pursue other endeavors.

The railroad made Sacramento a major transportation and commercial center in the west. Historian Theodore H. Hittel wrote, ". . . the sight of . . . armies of Chinese road builders completely organized . . . like thoroughly drilled troops . . . was a spectacle not to be forgotten."[7] Unfortunately, they were most often remembered as the curse of California's labor problems. Historical recognition of the contributions of the Chinese to California development were only too rare. The few compliments made were lost in a tide of anti-Chinese hysteria and rhetoric.

HUNG LAI WOH

Hung Lai Woh and his brother were among the thousands of Chinese who responded to the call for workers on America's first transcontinental railroad. They came from the village of Dai Long in Sum Hop (San He) Toishan. Many men from Dai Long left for Gum Saan to find work and it became known as the "village of foreign Chinese."

Hung Lai Woh was about fifteen years old when he and his older brother left for Hong Kong where they were herded into the steerage of a Pacific steamship along with hundreds of other Chinese recruited for the Central Pacific Railroad. They were headed to "Gold Mountain" and their destination was to a place they never heard of – the Sierra Nevada mountain region.

After a month and a half voyage across the Pacific Ocean, the steamer landed in San Francisco. The passengers were loaded onto boats bound for Sacramento and then onward to the Sierras. The brothers worked on the construction for snow sheds. Accidents and deaths were common. In one of the many blasting accidents, Lai Woh's brother lost an eye.

Following his work with the Central Pacific, Lai Woh returned home and returned to San Francisco in 1871. In 1888 he married Tom Ying, a young woman from the Presbyterian Occidental Home for Girls (Cameron House) and raised a family of five. Today, Hung Lai Woh and Tom Ying have over 100 descendants who live in the United States.

Left to right: Chun Ngou, Ah Gwei, Tom Shee, Kim Tun, Hung Lai Woh, Bing Quong, Kim Seung. (Story and photo courtesy of Russell Lowe, great grandson of Huang Lai Woh)

Chinese tent scene, at night, on the California Pacific Railroad, Sacramento Valley. June 11, 1870. (Author's collection)

Following the completion of the transcontinental railroad, a railroad boom commenced in California. The Chinese, now adept at drilling and blasting, became even more valuable as railroad workers.

They were employed by the California Pacific Railroad Company, which connected Sacramento with Vallejo. Steamer connection between Vallejo and San Francisco made this the only water and rail route between San Francisco and Sacramento.

THE MODERN ST. GEORGE

(Courtesy of the Chinese Historical Society of America)

(Courtesy of the Chinese Historical Society of America)

Labor's grievance was against the land barons who monopolized the land, and the railroad companies that monopolized transportation. These monopolistic interests were believed to be in league with the Chinese. Chinese "cheap" labor was blamed for all the problems of the white working class.

THE NEW COMET—A PHENOMENON NOW VISIBLE IN ALL PARTS OF THE UNITED STATES.

(Author's collection)

CHAPTER SIX

The Great Divide

BIGLER THE BIGOT AND OTHERS

No factor played so prominent a part in the history of California's labor movement as the presence of the Chinese. There were objections to the Chinese performing menial labor as houseboys and servants, claiming they were taking jobs away from young girls and women. However, it was their competition in mining, railroad building, agriculture, and light industries that brought on the most vociferous resentment. In the conflict between capital and labor, anti-monopoly sentiments quickly escalated into anti-Chinese hysteria. Some discontented laborers cursed the railroad giants and others damned the pro-Chinese politicians, but they all turned their bitter hostility into violent attacks on the Chinese.

In an era of rampant sinophobia, local and state government passed laws that, while facially neutral, clearly had a disparate impact on the Chinese. Laws were enacted to limit the ability of the Chinese to work, and to impose discriminatory taxes—all intended to exclude and to drive the Chinese from the state.

When legislation failed to diminish the presence of the Chinese, the discontented often resorted to violence. Mass "sandlot" rallies exhorted that "The Chinese must go," and were often followed by riots that destroyed local Chinatowns and resulted in injury and death. Moreover, violence against the Chinese often could be exacted with im-

punity because even if caught, rioters seldom were punished. Law enforcement did little to protect the Chinese. The courts would not allow Chinese to testify against whites, making attempts to obtain justice in the courts a near-futile endeavor.

Denis Kearny has been recorded in history as the infamous anti-Chinese demagogue who coined the phrase, "The Chinese Must Go!" during the 1877 sandlot riots in San Francisco, but it was Governor John Bigler who sounded the first alarm condemning the Chinese as a growing evil. In his message to the Legislature on April 23, 1852, Bigler warned, ". . . measures must be adopted to check the tide of Asiatic immigration and prevent the exploitation of them . . . the precious metal . . . from our soil . . . immigration must be limited to the Caucasian race." In 1855 he attacked the Chinese again and asked for a head tax on Asiatic immigration.

The 1850 Foreign Miner's Tax, which originally targeted the Mexicans, South Americans, and French, was reenacted in 1852 to also target the Chinese and discourage Chinese competition in the mother lode. In 1853, the tax was increased from two dollars to three dollars a month. A provision in the tax specifically required that it be translated into Chinese, Spanish, and French. Tong Achik, chairman of the Yeong Wo Association, translated the tax law into Chinese. Tong Achik had attended the Morrison

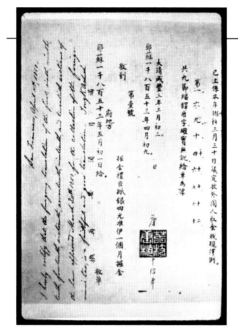

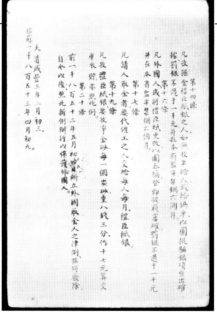

The 1850 Foreign Miner's Tax was reenacted in 1852 to discourage Chinese competition.

Tong Achik's seal and signature.

Articles 14 to 20.

Missionary School in Macao and had a perfect command of English.

Bigler's anti-Chinese message spread rapidly and advanced to the point where anyone who expected to hold political office was wise to denounce the Chinese. The "Chinese Question" formed a part of every message and every political platform for years. At every session, legislators endeavored to pass laws so oppressive that it would forbid or discourage Chinese immigration.

Leland Stanford took office on January 10, 1862, and in his inauguration speech he echoed Bigler's anti-Chinese policy, "that the presence of . . . that degraded and distinct people (who) would exercise a deleterious influence upon the superior race . . . it would therefore . . . afford him great pleasure to repress the immigration of Asiatic races." This despite the fact that the governor himself employed Chinese in his own household. Jin Mun worked as a gardener in the governor's mansion and Jin's brother worked as a cook. Furthermore, by the completion of the

transcontinental line by the Central Pacific Railroad, the Big Four had employed twelve thousand Chinese laborers. Ironically, Stanford's success and those of the other members of the Big Four had been in no small part due to the Chinese who had built their railroad.

Among the governors of California, only Governor Frederick F. Low, who was inaugurated on December 10, 1863, was elected without embarking on an anti-Chinese platform. Perhaps his early apprenticeship to the China trade East India firm of Russell, Sturgis and Company in Boston, gave him a different perspective. Upon leaving office he took a strong position against racial bigotry in defense of the Chinese. At the January 1867 commemoration of the establishment of a steamship line with China, he said, "We must . . . treat the Chinese who come to live among us decently, and not oppress them by unfriendly legislation . . ."[1]

In the gubernatorial election of 1867, candidates for governor had to declare their position on Chinese immigration. Candidate

George C. Gorham had the moral courage and integrity to declare his opposition to the anti-Chinese movement. Gorham unfortunately lost to Henry H. Haight, who proclaimed the white man desirable as a permanent population in California.[2]

Even as California's working men were campaigning against the presence of the Chinese, Congress in 1868 concluded a bilateral amendment to the Treaty of Tientsin, recognizing the right of man to freely emigrate "from one country to the other for purposes of . . . trade . . . or as permanent residents." This amendment was known as the Burlingame Treaty, and was exactly the opposite of the demands of the California representatives. The passage of this treaty enraged labor in California, and heightened anti-Chinese hysteria. For the next decade, outraged anti-Chinese mobs focused on the abrogation of the treaty. Governor Haight lost his bid for reelection in September 1871 when he betrayed the working men of California by presiding over a dinner reception for the Burlingame Party.[3]

Subsequent governors William Irwin and George Stoneman echoed traditional anti-Chinese rhetoric and emphasized the necessity of abrogating the Burlingame Treaty. Throughout the Pacific states, numerous anti-Chinese meetings and conventions existed over four decades up to the time of Governor Henry Gage, who echoed the same litany of protest in 1901.

Both political parties adopted an anti-Chinese plank to insure their political success. (Author's collection)

PANDERING TO SINOPHOBIA

The Workingmen's Alliance of Sacramento was formed on March 11, 1873. On May 29, 1873, the Workingmen's Alliance joined with the Anti-Chinese League of San Francisco and the Industrial Reformers to create a single organization, the People's Protective Alliance. This alliance united all of the anti-Chinese associations in the state into one central body. The only condition of membership to the alliance was to pledge to not vote for any political candidate who was not opposed to Chinese immigration.[4]

Communities took desperate measures to harass the Chinese. Laundries were easy and susceptible targets. In Sacramento, the Chi-

VOL. XLVIII No. 1241   PUCK BUILDING, New York, December 19th, 1900   PRICE TEN CENTS.
Copyright 1900 by Keppler & Schwarzmann

Entered at N. Y. P. O. as Second-class Mail Matter.

THE ULTIMATE CAUSE.

The contradiction between religious tenets and
immigration policies did not go unnoticed.
(Author's collection)

"THE MOUNTAIN IN LABOR."
(AESOP'S FABLES.)

As the conflict between labor and capital
increased, anti-Chinese rhetoric and
propaganda intensified on the West
Coast. The people formed anti-Chinese
organizations and held anti-Chinese mass
meetings. Governor Perkins proclaimed
March 4, 1882, a legal holiday for anti-
Chinese demonstrations.

(Author's collection)

nese took in laundry and washed it behind their houses in Sutter Lake (aka China Slough). They then laid the clothes on the rooftops to dry. The houses fronting on the north side of I Street extended on stilts over the lake on the backside.

Sacramento lawmakers passed an ordinance on October 6, 1876, that prohibited washing in the open air and required all laundry to be done indoors. Furthermore, Sacramento passed an ordinance that buildings extending over the water may not be used for occupancy. State legislators conspired with the unruly mob by passing numerous pieces of legislation, constitutional or not. Sacramento held proceedings on April 4, 1876, before a Senate Committee to document the evil presence of the Chinese and their effect on the social and political condition of the state, followed by a memorial to Congress pleading to be rescued. Enclosed with the memorial were essays and addresses by some of California's most prestigious and learned citizens. The General Association of Congregational Churches and Ministers of California condemned mob outrages, recommended churches evangelize those Chinese already present in the state, but nevertheless expressed the conviction that measures be adopted to restrict Chinese immigration. An address by John H. Boalt, member of the San Francisco Bar, stressed, "the physical peculiarities and intellectual differences make assimilation impossible."

Increasing propaganda and violence compelled Congress to finally take action. The Senate, on July 6, 1876, and the House, on July 17, 1876, appointed a joint committee to investigate the grievances and disturbances coming from the Pacific states. The committee took testimony from 130 witnesses and produced a voluminous report of over 1,200 pages. The committee found: "Chinese cheap labor had been responsible for the rapid development of the resources of the Pacific Coast but looking toward the future, many people of the Pacific Coast believe that this influx of the Chinese . . . who show few of the characteristics of a desirable population . . . must be restrained. Measures must be taken to modify the existing treaty strictly to commercial purposes."

Depression in the state during the 1870s was further aggravated by the immigrant associations enticing the unemployed from the East with promises of the Golden West. The ranks of the white unemployed swelled. Chinese labor competition was blamed yet again. The railroad "barons" dominated government and transportation. Land ownership and water rights fell into the hands of a few. Corporations, especially banks, were not accountable to the public.

Under the newly-adopted 1879 California Constitution, discrimination was institutionalized. The Chinese Question was unabashedly dealt with under Article XIX of the Constitution, which provided no corporation "shall employ...any Chinese. No Chinese shall be employed on any state, county, municipal or other public work except for punishment for crime. Legislature shall delegate all necessary power to cities and towns . . . for the removal of Chinese . . ."

Despite blatantly harsh and federally unconstitutional provisions, the new California Constitution failed to achieve its objectives. The railroads continued to use Chinese labor in its expansion throughout the western states. Other corporations also continued to employ Chinese. It was clear that total exclusion had to come from Congress.

EXCLUSION ACTS

Members of Congress from the Pacific states continued their efforts to bring forth the Chinese Question as their chief political issue. Finally, the President appointed a commission to negotiate a new treaty with China. The treaty in November 17, 1880, permitted the United States to regulate, limit, or suspend immigration of Chinese laborers. The new treaty negated the provision for ". . . free migration and emigration of their citizens . . . from one country to the other . . ." and cleared the way for the United States to introduce a bill to suspend Chinese immigration. To encourage public acceptance of the passage of the Exclusion Act, Governor George C. Perkins declared Saturday, March 4, 1882, a legal holiday for anti-Chinese demonstrations.[5] The Exclusion Act passed on May 6, 1882, and provided for the exclusion of skilled and unskilled laborers for a period of ten years. Yet the passage of the Exclusion Act did little to placate the still discontented public.

In concert with the State Constitution, Article XIX, which gave the Legislature the power to remove the Chinese, Sacramento's Ordinance Committee attempted to remove the Chinese quarters and the Chinese from within the city limits. A bill drafted by Grove L. Johnson, Chairman of the Board, was submitted to the Board of Trustees. The Board asked Hon. A. P. Catlin for his legal opinion. Judge Catlin responded with a display of integrity rare for the times, ". . . the proposed ordinance by reason of its application to Chinese exclusively, would fall dead beneath the weight of the fourteenth amendment."[6] Citing the articles in the treaty with China, "the Chinese are guaranteed the same rights that other aliens are." Thwarted by the judge's opinion, the Citizen's Anti-Chinese Organization of Sacramento merged with the nine county Non-Partisan Anti-Chinese Association to establish a permanent organization called the California Anti-Chinese Non-partisan Association. Another memorial to Congress was sent on March 11, 1886, containing the usual anti-Chinese rhetoric.

Even as America closed its doors to Chinese immigration, American lawmakers pushed for even more access to China and its resources. On September 6, 1899, Secretary of State John Hay declared the policy of an "Open Door" to China. Notes were transmitted to England, France, Italy, Germany, Russia, and Japan; their purpose was to affirm equal commercial opportunities among the nations, including the building of railroads, the opening of mines, and industrial exploitation in China. While pursuing an open door policy to China, the United States blatantly ignored their pledges of "mutual respect" and "reciprocal immigration" with China.

The Exclusion Act of May 1882 suspended the immigration of Chinese laborers for ten years. In 1902, exclusion was made indefinite, violating the Treaty of 1880, which provided for temporary exclusion. The exclusion acts were effective in slowing down immigration, but did not absolutely stop the coming of the Chinese to the United States. While Congress was busy making amendments to plug the loopholes in the exclusion law, the Chinese were finding loopholes to immigrate. The courts were still faced with the task of adjudicating the immigration rights of individual Chinese.

THERE'S MILLIONS IN IT.

Despite widespread anti-Chinese sentiment and criticism, the courts under Judge Ogden Hoffman (Northern District Court) and Justice Lorenzo Sawyer (Ninth Circuit), insisted on allowing individual Chinese to present evidence regarding their rights to be in the United States. State and federal officials, the media, and the public accused them of "creating loopholes" in legislation restricting immigration. The many thousands of Chinese *habeas corpus* cases caused Judge Sawyer to complain in an 1888 letter to a colleague that "we are buried out of sight in Chinese *habeas corpus* cases." While Justice Sawyer wrote of the "industrious" Chinese, Judge Hoffman often exhorted the need for federal legislation to prevent Chinese immigration, which he thought to "menace our interest, our safety, and even our civilization." Despite their personal beliefs, Judge Hoffman and Justice Sawyer often struck down legislation arising from anti-Chinese sentiment. (Author's collection)

BAPTIST
CHINESE MISSION.
浸信會

*Many people in
America have never
seen a Chinese child . . .
they speak English . . .
they are far more
American than Chinese.*

M. E. Church, *Understanding the
Oriental Americans*, 1930

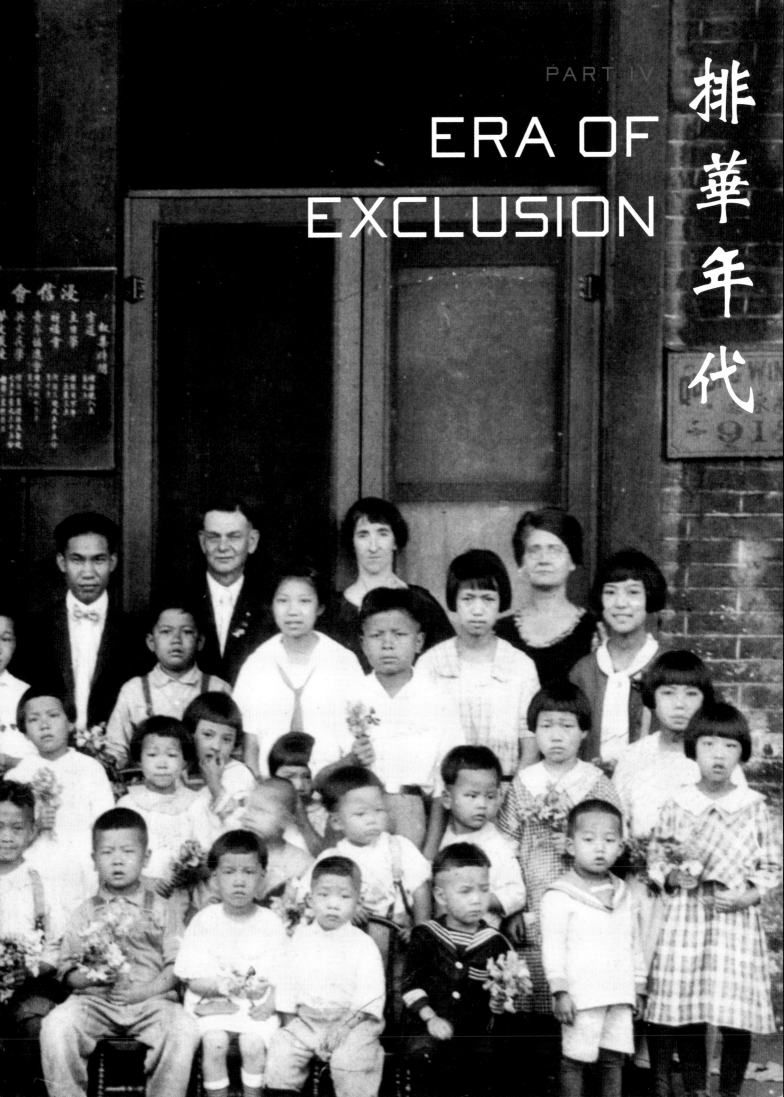

PART IV

ERA OF EXCLUSION

排華年代

The "Open Door Policy" pronounced by Secretary of State John Hay in 1899 to insure the United States received its share of commerce with China. (Author's collection)

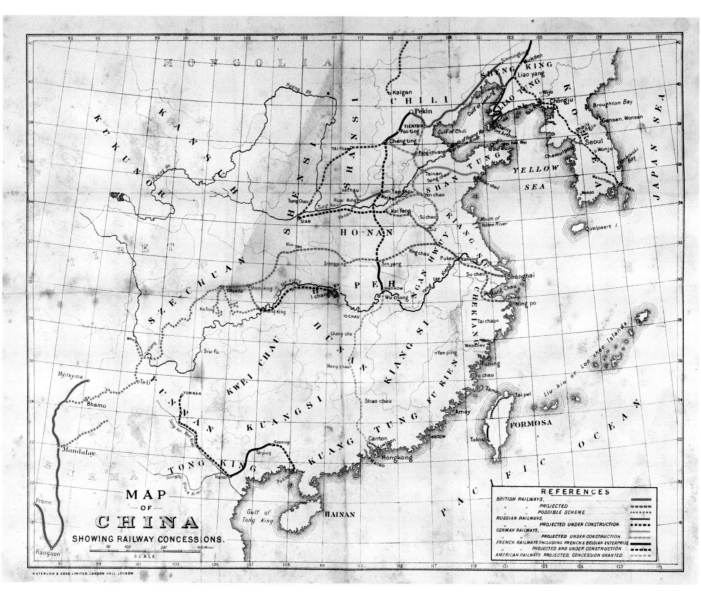

Map circa 1898. Besides securing territorial concessions, foreign countries competed for the rights to build, control, and operate railroads and develop mines along its right of way. (Author's collection)

CHAPTER SEVEN

Emigration and Immigration Restrictions

JAPAN'S AGGRESSION

From the time of the Opium War to World War II, China did not experience any significant periods of peace. By the end of the nineteenth century, the threat to the sovereignty of China was not only from the West but also from her neighbor Japan. The morale of the population was at a new low. The Chinese continued to immigrate in spite of the passage of the exclusion acts.

The intent of Commodore Matthew Perry's expedition in 1853 was to open the doors to Japan and to expand U.S. influence and power in Asia. Instead, a monster was born and unleashed, and in a span of less than fifty years, Japan emerged from an age of feudalism to become a major industrial and military power, challenging the presence of western nations in Asia. She assumed the self-serving and self-appointed role of protectorate of China's territorial integrity.

Beginning in 1874, Japan embarked on a course of aggression resulting in the occupation of Formosa (Taiwan), the annexation of Korea, and after the defeat of Russia in 1904, acquisition of Manchuria. For over six decades Japan continued to pursue a course of conquest in Asia.

Two political groups at the end of the nineteenth century emerged and sought to salvage China from partition by foreign exploitation. The followers of K'ang Yu-wei promoted a policy of reforming the Manchu monarchy while Dr. Sun Yat-Sen advocated

revolution to oust the imperial dynasty.

Dr. Sun's revolution succeeded, but with the defeat of the Manchu, China's problems had just begun. The revolution brought freedom from three hundred years of Manchu rule yet the euphoria was short-lived. Feudal warlords held various parts of China and fought for sovereignty over the whole country. Chaos and confusion followed.

Japan felt it necessary to step up her aggression before China could awaken and unify. The Japanese bribed feuding Chinese warlords by setting up puppet governments in Japanese occupied territory.

The Japanese occupied harbors along the mainland, raped and plundered as they conducted military forays into Shanghai, Nanking, and Hankow. They continued to set up puppet governments under Japanese control. By the fall of 1938, the city of Canton, under siege, finally fell under Japanese occupation. The accumulation of misfortune begun in the mid-nineteenth century pushed China into anarchy and poverty by the early twentieth

One-hundred-three-year-old Benny Woon Yep.

century. To this day Chinese still greet each other rhetorically, "Have you eaten yet?" The phrase stems from the concern for the lack of food throughout a century of poverty and starvation from political disorder and economic instability.

Benny Woon Yep, who emigrated at the age of thirteen recalled, "When you're in China . . . you got nothing to do. Anybody got money is people who come to the United States. All I know . . . a lot of Chinese did their best to come to the United States to try to find gold."

The Chinese from Guangdong continued to seek passage to the Gold Mountain to find relief from political strife and poverty. Unfortunately, passage of the Exclusion Act of 1882 ended the period of free immigration, and an era of restrictive immigration followed.

DECEPTION AND ADMISSION DENIED

Under the Chinese exclusion laws, the coming of Chinese laborers to the United States was absolutely prohibited, and no Chinese were admitted to citizenship. The only classes exempted from exclusion were diplomats, merchants, teachers, students, or travelers for curiosity or pleasure. Merchants and their wives and minor children were exempted in order to honor the reciprocal trade and commercial provisions of treaties. For decades Chinese devised extralegal means to circumvent the exclusion laws.

A popular means was to take advantage of the exempt merchant classification by investing in a business. Laundries, fishing, and restaurants were not included in the permissible category of business. Under the merchant classification, wives and minor children of merchants were permitted to immigrate. All foreign-born children of United States citizens were citizens by derivation. Therefore purchasing the birthright of a son or a daughter of a merchant or a citizen and adopting their identity was another common method of immigration. This arrangement was known as the "paper father and paper son."

The denial to citizenship and immigration for Chinese women was specifically regulated with the passage of the Cable Act of 1922 and the Immigration Act of 1924. In the Cable Act, an American woman would lose her citizenship by marrying an alien "ineligible for citizenship." This was directed at Chinese women because the Chinese were declared ineligible for citizenship under the Exclusion Act of 1882. In the Immigration Act of 1924, Chinese wives of American citizens were not permitted to immigrate except if they were married before the passage of the Act. The alien wife of a merchant had more rights than an American-born Chinese wife.

Chinese attempting to enter the United States as children of citizens or as merchants were generally boys in their teens, mature enough to assume responsibility for earning a living. Their first obligation was to pay off the debt owed to the person who brokered the paper father and paper son connection, and then to make enough to support himself and the family back home.

From 1903 to 1908, a period of five years, the number admitted as wives of merchants was 155, as children of merchants was 1,900, and as children of American-born was 4,535. United States Commissioner General of

Bert Fong (aka Fong Sui) and his wife
(Courtesy of Bobby Fong)

Chan Tai Oy and Tung Lin Leong
(Courtesy of Dan Chan, Jr.)

Under the classification of "wife of a merchant," Mrs. Bert Fong was permitted to enter the United States. On the other hand, Tung Lin Leong, born in Madera, California, lost her citizenship under the Cable Act of 1922 by marrying Chan Tai Oy, an "alien ineligible for citizenship." When she left the country in 1929, she re-entered as the wife of a merchant.

Bureau of Immigration Terence V. Powderly, former head of the Knights of Labor, pledged total exclusion of the Chinese and boasted, ". . . whatever is done, the Chinese will be kept out."[1] He appointed James R. Dunn as Chinese Inspector at San Francisco. Dunn, a former union man, was equally enthusiastic in executing the exclusion laws. Thus while the Chinese were devising every possible means of deception to immigrate, the main thrust of the Bureau was directed at denying admission of all Chinese to the United States. For decades a "cat and mouse" game existed between the Bureau and the Chinese immigrants.

The May 18, 1906, report from the Secretary of Commerce to the House of Representatives, entitled Enforcement of the Chinese Exclusion Laws, pointed out that ". . . the Chinese gain unlawful access to this country by constantly declaring to be merchants . . . firms having the aggregate of $1,000.00 in value in one year would have membership of from 10 to 30 persons each claiming

to have $500.00 or $1,000.00 invested. When . . . such firm is visited, no more than two or three . . . are found . . . the purposes for which these firms are organized are so obvious . . ."[2]

To detect fraudulent claims of being a merchant, I. B. Sawyer, American Vice Consul in Shanghai, issued a Manual of Procedures that recommended "surprise" visits to the place of business, and conducting a series of tests by going over the firm's records to verify the merchant was familiar with its major transactions. The manual required the merchant to demonstrate his skill with working the abacus as proof of his business acumen.[3]

A person going back to China but intending to return had to file a "pre-investigation of status" with the Commissioner of Immigration.[4] This was to prove his status as a bona fide member of one of the exempt classes before the permit was issued. The process entailed extensive interrogation.

Prior to the Exclusion Act of 1882, Chinese businesses flourished in response to the burgeoning mining, reclamation, agriculture, and railroad population. The 1882 Wells Fargo Directory listed sixteen merchant businesses. A 1901 unidentified directory listed twenty-six businesses and in 1913, that number almost doubled.[5]

The attempt to ferret out fraudulent claims by surprise visits had little impact on the businesses as evidenced by the increase in the number of businesses that flourished. The presence of fifth and sixth generation Sacramentans today is testimony to the tenacity of the Chinese, surviving in spite of systematic harassment by the Bureau of Immigration.

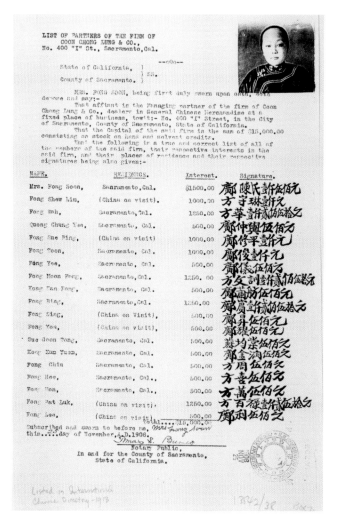

The names of the partners were also registered in Chinese.

Merchants, Paper Merchants, Fathers and Paper Sons

LINCOLN MARKET

Lincoln Market was established by Fong Yue Po in 1912. A photograph of the shop in 1927 showed seven members in an apparently modest size grocery store. Yet in 1918, they filed with the immigration service a partnership list of twenty-two partners and twenty-one silent partners.

The daughter of Fong Yue Po, Virginia Chan, in an interview said, "Father started the store so he can help friends come to the United States." Fong came to the United States in 1908 at the age of nineteen by adopting the identity of the son of his aunt and uncle. His grandfather was here in the 1880s and his grand uncle managed to arrange the immigration for two of his brothers. However, a fourth brother was denied admission so he bribed his way as a stowaway aboard a ship. He jumped ship after the ship docked in San Diego and took a coach to Sacramento. A system of stations existed from Mexico through California to assist illegal immigrants from point to point.[6]

Fong first worked on tomato farms in Stockton, then went to Sacramento and worked in restaurants, hotels, and grocery stores. His activities with the politics of China—casting off the yoke of the Manchu rule—inspired him to name his store Lincoln Market with the portrait of Abraham Lincoln on the letterhead. He equated the freedom of slavery with the Chinese freedom from three hundred years of Manchu rule.

Lincoln Market illustrates how the Chinese frustrated immigration officials. This photograph taken in 1927 shows seven members in a modest size shop. Yet in 1918, the manager filed with the immigration service a partnership list of twenty-two partners and twenty-one silent partners. (Courtesy of Virginia [Fong] Chan)

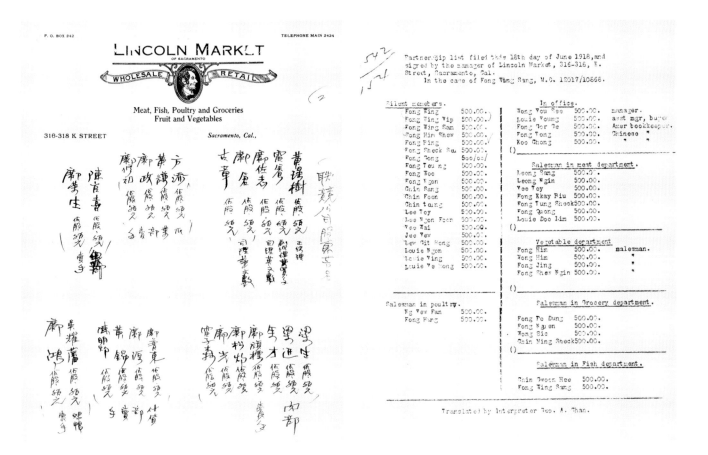

TONG SUNG

The Bureau of Immigration assumed all Chinese operated their businesses as a front for illegal immigration. But while the Chinese often exploited the exempt status of merchants to its fullest to facilitate immigration, the businesses were actually legitimate and provided the means for earning a living. Raising capital to start a business by soliciting funds from friends and relatives was a common practice. In the hope of increasing opportunities for accumulating wealth, the owners of a business would invest as silent partners in new firms. Dong Haw, major owner of Hong King Lum Restaurant, also invested as a silent partner in Liberty Meat Market. Fong Chuck, major owner of Capitol Poultry and Fish invested in Farmer's Market, Wonder Food, and General Food. Many firms like Tong Sung had been established even before the exclusion act. From time to time Tong Sung had as many as thirty partners, both active and silent. In fifty years of operation it had accounts throughout the United States and shipped products as far east as Minnesota. At one time it was doing business with 278 firms, of which 85 were in the city of Sacramento. These included major clientele such as the Hotel Senator, F.W. Woolworth, and S.F. Depot Restaurant.

In 1894 the store had six partners: Soon Chip, Chun Mow Tong, Chun Chong, Tung Bing, and Chun Wing. Each held a five hundred dollar interest, and Chun Sing, the manager, held a two thousand dollar interest. In 1923 it grew to 9 active partners and 10 silent partners in China.

Chan Tai Oy came to the United States on February 20, 1905 as the paper son of merchant Chan Jock Chee, who was here since 1870 at age twenty-two. Jock Chee was really his uncle. He passed the usually rigorous interrogation but was denied entry because the medical examiner reported he had trachoma, a disease considered dangerous at that time. On October 24, 1905, he applied again and this time was permitted to enter the United States. When Tai Oy arrived, Jock Chee sold him half of his share of the business for two thousand dollars. Tai Oy started at Tong Sung as a cook and by 1908 had become manager of the firm until the business closed its doors in 1933.

After thirty-five years of operation, Tong Sung went bankrupt and closed its doors. With the financial backing of brother-in-law Jue Chong, inventor of the asparagus plow, Tai Oy and his son, Eddie restarted the business in 1933. Conscious of being American, Eddie suggested using the name General Produce in lieu of a Chinese name. As Eddie's brothers, Daniel and Thomas grew older, they joined the business. Today, General Produce is a multi-million dollar business under the management of grandsons Dan Chan, Jr., and Tommy Chan, Jr.

Tong Sung was established before 1881. The company had six partners in 1894, and at one time had as many as thirty active and silent partners.

(Courtesy of Dan Chan, Jr.)

Tong Sung in 1910. Left to right: Look Chong, Chan Tai Oy, Leong [Jaing or Jiang] Lee, Chan Sik Lee (Courtesy of Dan Chan, Jr.)

Chan Tai Oy and son Eddie. (Courtesy of Dan Chan, Jr.)

After almost fifty years of being in business, Tong Sung went bankrupt. Tai Oy and his son Eddie restarted the business. Eddie suggested using the name of General Produce in lieu of a traditional Chinese name. (Author's collection)

WING LEE MEAT MARKET

To establish one's right to stay in the United States as a legitimate merchant was a complex process and a simple mistake could jeopardize the right of entry or re-entry. Howard Jan of Wing Lee Meat Market experienced such a difficulty in his youth.

Howard's father Jan Wai, and his uncle Jan Wy, with other partners established Wing Lee Meat Market in 1913. Jan Wai came to the United States in 1882 and worked as a merchant with See Hop Company at 1009 Dupont Street in San Francisco.

Jan Wai married Lin Look in San Francisco on June 26, 1903 and lived at 752 Pacific Street where Jung Yuet Ngan (Eleanor) and Gee Hin (Henry) were born. After the 1906 earthquake, the family went to China where Howard and John were born. Jan Wai returned to the United States first and the family, except daughter Eleanor who was left behind, later returned as the paper wife and sons of a merchant.

Henry was sent to China to study and upon returning from China in 1927, he was taken ill and was put ashore at Honolulu.

Howard was sent to bring him back. Because of the emergency, Howard neglected to bring his certificate of identification, and did not file a report with the Bureau of Immigration to establish his right to return. Howard only had a statement by a notary public certifying his identity. Before the passage of the exclusion acts, the Chinese had already migrated to Hawaii in large numbers. All exclusion acts were applicable to the territory of Hawaii. The immigration officer in Hawaii would not issue him the right to land nor the right to return to the United States. Howard was detained on Angel Island pending interrogation. Perhaps confident he was raised American or perhaps naive and unaware of the immigration officer's hostile stance, Howard agreed to waive his rights to a hearing to allow witnesses' admission of documentation. He was denied immediate admission but the committee agreed to defer his case pending investigation. After ten days the information gathered did ascertain Howard was a bona fide domiciled merchant at Wing Lee and he was finally released.

Wing Lee Meat Company was established by Jan Wai in 1913 at 1122 Third Street. Left to right: Harry Jan, Howard Jan, David Jan peeking between the narcissus plants, unknown, Peter Jan, unknown, Jan Hin Mun, Leung Fook, Jan Wei

Unknown to, or perhaps forgotten by the generations following the exclusion acts, the Chinese in the nineteenth century were major contributors to the development of California's agriculture. Some of the immigrants following exclusion continued this farming tradition. While they were admitted under the merchant class, once they gained entry they would enter into whatever employment was available even though changing one's status meant deportation if discovered and challenged. Chinese tenant farming continued to be a common livelihood.

In 1900, Sacramento County had 231 farmers working 1,032 acres with 1,165 Chinese farm laborers. According to the 1910 Immigration Commission Report, nearly every ranch visited was found to have been leased to the same tenant who leased it year after year. When the original lessors died or returned to China, sons came to replace them.

By the second decade of the twentieth century, families began to appear. In the 1999 reunion of former residents of the Sacramento Delta, ninety persons responded to a survey—seventy-four were born in the delta region, ten in China, four in San Francisco, and three in Sacramento.[7]

HING HUNG OWYANG

Dr. Hing Owyang, Jr.'s father immigrated in 1904 as a merchant, and after working in San Francisco five years he went to Courtland. He remained with the Runyon and Dorsey Ranch for forty-seven years and raised six children. The oldest child, Qui Yin, was born in China, and Jon, Elsie, Laura, George, and Hing Jr. were born on the ranch.

Runyon and Dorsey Ranch

Hing Hung Owyang's real surname was Jang. His father immigrated by purchasing the identity of a merchant named Ow Young Hong Hing, a partner with the firm of Sang Wo Sang at 613 Jackson Street in San Francisco. His uncle, Ow Young Lin You, who had been here for a number of years, advised him to apply for citizenship by claiming his birth certificate was destroyed during the 1906 earthquake. Hong Hing was successful in obtaining a "certificate of birth" document but chose not to take advantage of his status as a citizen. In 1909, after working five years at Sang Wo Sang he was ready to return home to seek a wife. Because he entered the country as a merchant it was advisable to leave and return under the same status. While at home he married and fathered a baby girl. Leaving his wife and baby behind he returned to the United States, but reported the birth of a son instead of a daughter. When he finally sent for his daughter, she had to come as the daughter of another citizen, Jang Kim.

While he did not use his citizenship status for reasons unknown, neither did he use his merchant status to advantage. When his wife, Shun Dai, joined him in 1916, she entered as the wife of his brother, Jang On, who purportedly was a citizen. When in 1936, eighteen-year-old daughter Elsie applied to study in China, each member of the family had to appear before the Bureau of Immigration to undergo interrogation, even twelve-year-old Hong Jr. Complications arose as to the marriage of the parents. Hong Hing had recorded he had a wife in China when he first immigrated. How was it that he had a wife here? Furthermore, Shun Dai was admitted as the wife of Jang On! What was going on here? Apparently the family was forewarned and prepared for the interrogation. The story fabricated was his first wife and family all perished in China in 1917, and in 1918 he took in Shun Dai when Jang On abandoned her. The officials accepted the convoluted explanation, but they were required to legalize their marriage in accordance to American laws.

JANG GAY SUN AND GRAND ISLAND

Jang Gay Sun, a native of Chung Shan, immigrated to the United States after the 1906 San Francisco earthquake. His father was here during the era of the gold rush. He proceeded to Courtland in the Sacramento delta where his brother, Jang Gay Hin, was a tenant farmer, half a mile south of Courtland. Gay Hin's farm was named On Sang Yuen. Gay Sun started farming on Grand Island by leasing sixty acres from W. J. Smith of Pacific Food: he named his farm Yick Sang Yuen. About 1908, his wife joined him and on Grand Island they raised a family of five boys, Tim, Edwin, Edward, Joe, Edgar, and five girls, Wynne, Lina, Lily, Ruby, and Betty. Their neighbor tenant farmers were Lee Tin Fook and Warren Lai.

Jang Gay Sun leased the farm until he passed away in 1962 and his son, Edwin continued on through the 1960s. Fortuitously, Gay Sun, Hong Hing and fellow tenant farmers in the Sacramento delta were continuing a long history of farming stemming back to the early 1850s. On Grand Island, Brannan Island, and Sherman Island, the tenant farming system prevailed with the Chinese predominating as tenants and laborers until the exclusion acts reduced their numbers. Thereafter, Italian and Portuguese farmers came, with the Japanese ultimately outnumbering the Chinese as well. While Gay Sun sharecropped acres of pears, peaches, plums, and apples, the farmers south of Courtland devoted tracts of land for the production of asparagus, another major crop in the early decades of the twentieth century. The Sacramento delta became eventually renown as the asparagus capital of the world.

JUE CHONG AND THE ASPARAGUS PLOW

Clearing the land after harvesting the asparagus was a backbreaking job. The old roots with their large rhizomes spread no less then eight feet across. Farmers would replant the crop over and over again without clearing the field of old plants. With each replanting, the crop would diminish and yield less and less. With the invention of Jue Chong's asparagus plow, the old root and plants would be ground up finely and churned over leaving the soil ready for replanting. Jue and Tony Miller made their money by contracting their services for plowing asparagus fields after the harvest.

Jue and his siblings were all born in Madera, California, where their father farmed, but the business was not doing well. Following the father's death in 1916, the older brothers Lee Chong, Jue, and Sam went to Ryde, California, and continued to farm while the two younger brothers, Bing and Luk, went to school in Sacramento. They stayed with their brother-in-law, Chan Tai Oy, who was married to their sister, Tung Lin Leong.

The brothers raised beets, pears, peaches, and onions; and the farming proved to be rewarding. With the fruits of his success, Lee did what he loved best with the money—he bought and drove the latest model automobile. Nephew Eddie Chan remembered, ". . . when the fleet came into San Francisco he took all of us out in his big car . . . and watch the fleet come in the Golden Gate. The bridge wasn't there then you know. That was in World War I."

Lee's extravagance wasn't all for himself. Perhaps mindful of his own hardship while farming in Madera, he took care of his workers by providing not only decent housing, with individual bedrooms and bathrooms—but complete with kitchen and a Chinese cook! This was contrary to the prevailing practice of housing laborers in squalid shacks. Eddie Chan marveled, "He took that money and built a big housing project on the same ranch for the workers in Ryde just like a motel. It's still there. He built that thing, looked like a motel."

However, Jue and Sam did not share their brother's lifestyle and parted ways. They partnered with Tony Miller on a ranch west of the Isleton Bridge. It was there in the 1920s the asparagus plow was invented by Jue and Tony.

Jue Chong and Tony Miller
(photograph by Al Avila)

QUONG FUNG

The activities of a few partners of the Quong Fung store demonstrate how the Chinese exploited and circumvented the Exclusion Act. They did not allow the restrictive regulations to trample their human spirit and stifle their business acumen. They went beyond the role of merchants and ventured into farming.

Fong Sik entered the country on July 14, 1900, at the age of twenty, under the exempt classification of a teacher, using the name Chan Yuen Chong. He became manager of Quong Fung in 1912. Sam Fong (aka Kwong Wing Haw) immigrated in 1910 at the age of eighteen as a student and named Fong Sik as his provider. In 1900, Fong Shee immigrated as a paper son by adopting the identity of sixteen-year-old Fong Shew Tang, the son of Fong Ben, a merchant of Lincoln Market. Fong Shee also became a partner in Quong Fung.

Before leaving for China to obtain a wife and to insure their return, each of these men qualified themselves as merchants of Quong Fung.

When Sam returned from China in 1917, he leased thirty acres of land along Linden Road in Yolo County and went into farming. Fong Sik took an interest in farming and asked Sam to join him in leasing some scrubland in Woodland. Sam contributed his knowledge and farm equipment from his Linden Road ranch. Fong Shee joined them and helped clear the land for raising sugar beets and tomatoes.

The Woodland venture was successful and when the lease terminated, Fong Sik and Sam bought 320 acres in Natomas. The farm was called Fong Ranch Company. State Market, where Fong Sik was manager, provided pro-

visions for the farming operations. The farm did well and Fong Sik shared the good fortune by giving shares of the business to the partners at State Market and the loyal workers on the Natomas farm.

The crops cultivated were alfalfa, barley, mung beans, celery, sugar beets, and tomatoes. The tomatoes went to Bercut Richards, a local cannery. Since the cannery had a limited capacity, they controlled the pace of processing by controlling the number of empty boxes to be filled by the growers. Each truckload held 508 boxes. Oftentimes William, the oldest son of Sam, would have to wait anxiously all night for empty boxes to be taken back to the ranch to be refilled. The sugar beets went to the Spreckel's Sugar refinery. The alfalfa was baled and sold to dairy farms in Marin County. According to William, who worked on the farm during this time, the labor was supplied by a Mexican labor contractor named Bill Barber, who picked up a mixed labor force, which included at that time some California Native Americans from the north coast and Lake County and an ethnically diverse group from Sacramento's skid row on Second Street. The irony is obvious as in the nineteenth century, the Chinese were the predominant agricultural laborers. During the height of the World War II years when there was a shortage of available labor, friends and neighbors became the sources of labor.

In 1942 and 1943, celery became an important crop. Roger, Sam's third son, described the celery growing and processing as a "neighborhood project." He and his brother Edward (aka Pee Wee), along with their friends (city boys unaccustomed to stoop labor), would work in the fields during

The activities of a few partners at Quong Fong demonstrates how the Chinese did not allow the restrictive regulations of the exclusion acts trample their human spirit and stifle their business acumen. (Courtesy of Lana Chong)

summer vacation. Some of them wore war-time steel helmets and planted celery for forty-five cents an hour. Roger said they didn't have portable toilets in the fields and the closest irrigation ditch had to do. He also recalled that during those scorching, one-hundred-plus degree days, their friends would quit working and walk to the American River to swim. He and his brother, Ed didn't go because their father, Sam was the foreman. During the fall harvest, friends of their mother would be recruited to work in the packing shed, washing, trimming, and boxing the celery in crates with their own blue and yellow "CAL STATE" label. Roger and Ed glued all the labels to the box slats during their free time.

The crates of celery were shipped by refrigerated boxcar to the East Coast and Canadian markets.

In the 1940s, the group purchased the Pearson Ranch along the Garden Highway and named it the Fong Sacramento Fruit Ranch. An additional thirty acres was purchased across the road from Fong Ranch and was named the Oy Ling Ranch. Fong Shee was given shares in the Fong Sacramento Fruit Ranch for his hard work.

Initially, Fong Sik maintained the books while the three farms were managed at various times either by Sam Fong or Fong Shee. Fong Sik did not farm. Usually on Sunday, Fong Sik would be driven to the farms by his

Fong Sik aka Chan Yuen Chong (Courtesy of Merrily Wong)

Fong Sik surveying his holdings with inner satisfaction. (Courtesy of Merrily Wong)

IN RE WONG ARK FUNG, A MERCHANT AND MEMBER OF THE FIRM OF
STATE MARKET.

STATE OF CALIFORNIA)
) SS.
COUNTY OF SACRAMENTO)

FONG HONG BING, whose photograph
is hereto attached, being first duly sown
deposes and says: That he is a member of
the co-partnership known as STATE MARKET,
which is a mercantile firm with its principal place of business at No. 430 M Street
in the City of Sacramento, County of Sacramento, State of California; that affiant
is and for more than two years last past
has been a member of said co-partnership and
during all of said time has been and is a
domiciled resident of the City of Sacramento, County of Sacramento,
State of California; that the names of the partners who constitute
said co-partnership of STATE MARKET and the amount of capital
invested by each of them in said co-partnership business are as
follows:

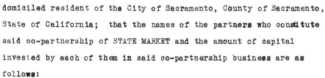

CHAN FONG SIK	陳若錫	Treasurer	$ 1000.00
KWONG CHUNG WO	鄺宗和	Bookkeeper	$ 500.00
FONG HONG BING	鄺鴻枋	Manager	$ 500.00
WONG ARK FUNG	黃德煥	Salesman	$ 500.00
FONG MON CHOW	鄺文超	Salesman	$ 500.00
WONG YOU KWONG	黃優光	Salesman	$ 500.00
LOUIE BOW	雷伴	Salesman	$ 500.00
FONG SHEU YUE	鄺隆霞	Salesman	$ 500.00
FONG SHEW TANG	鄺北祥	Silent	$ 500.00
FONG LIN GAR	鄺連家		$ 500.00
LOUIE HOK YIN	雷学仁		$ 500.00
WONG YEE JUN	黃宇進		$ 500.00

State Market managed by Fong Sik provided provisions for the Fong Ranch Company, Oy Ling Ranch and Fong Sacramento Fruit Ranch operations.

Sam Fong with his children William and Audrey Fong (Ah Tye) at the Linden Road farm, 1929. (Courtesy of Roger Fong)

daughter, Mary, and he would appear dressed in his business suit, tie, and hat. Gazing across the horizon, he would survey his holdings with inner satisfaction. The success of the farming operations was due largely to the collaborative efforts of the three men.

The farms were eventually all sold. Fong Ranch is now the site of the regional mall "The Promenade." Some of the land was purchased by the school district and a portion was gifted to the Natomas Senior High School, and the library was named in memory of the Fongs farming roots. The former Rosin Road leading to the school was renamed Fong Ranch Road.

Sam Fong immigrated with his cousin, Bert Fong (aka Kwong Yu Sui). Bert also immigrated under the exempt student classification in 1910. They had attended the German Catholic school in Tsingtau, Shantung, where Sam's father, Kwong Yi Shan was a furniture maker. They applied for visas to go to Holyoke, Massachusetts, for further education in mining and railroad engineering. There they would stay with Mrs. Daisie Dickenson, who lived at 157 Pleasant Street. En route, they claimed they would stay with their "uncle," Kwang King Lai (Fong Sik), manager at Quong Fung in Sacramento. Once landed in the United States though, neither boy continued their journey to Massachusetts, as declared.

Bert held various jobs, working at the Southern Pacific Railroad shops and yard, and selling fruit and produce door-to-door from his wagon, including chickens and pigs, until he saved enough to return home to obtain a wife. When Bert and his wife first arrived, they settled in West Sacramento, where relatives and a number of bachelors who worked for Southern Pacific, also lived. Bert's wife cooked for them, and during canning season, she worked in the cannery.

A friend offered Bert a vacant store where he opened Sheu Fung, his poultry shop. Bert and his wife lived in the back of the store. By the 1930s, they celebrated the opening of a new brick building that replaced the old wooden one. Sheu Fung was a local favorite and the business prospered. Much of the business came from the casinos in Reno, Nevada, where Chinese were in charge of the kitchens and ordered poultry from them. Sheu Fung was also a favorite stopping place of Governor Earl Warren. He would arrive in his hunting clothes after a hunting trip and drop off the ducks and geese to be dressed.

Sheu Fung was located in the heart of the redevelopment area in Sacramento and in 1958, the business closed. No one cared to continue the business in another location. As son Bobby said, "We've seen enough chickens in our days!"

Fong Shee's philosophy:
"Always I work."

Fong in his sixties and still enjoying the tilling of the soil at the Fong
Sacramento Fruit Ranch. (Photos courtesy of Lana Chong)

Sheu Fong, the new building in 1931. (Courtesy of Sacramento Archives and Museum Collection Center)

Sheu Fong, the old building in 1921. (Courtesy of Bobby Fong)

Sam Fong (aka Kwong Wing Haw) immigrated with his cousin Bert Fong (aka Kwong Yu Sui) under the exempt classification of student. They had attended the German Catholic School in Tsingtao, Shantung, where Sam's father was a furniture maker.

AMERICAN CONSULAR SERVICE,

Tsingtau, China October 22, 1909.

To the

Immigration Officer in Charge,

Port of San Francisco, Cal.

Sir:

I have the honor to enclose herewith copy of a letter from the Chefoo Consulate, and a precis of information regarding the evidence upon which a vise' was given on Chinese Section Six certificates issued by the Taotai of the Teng lai Ch'ing circuit of Chefoo, Shantung, China, to Kwang wing hau and Kwang yu sui, Chinese students who intend to enter the United States at your port.

Trusting you will give these boys every possible facility for landing,

I have the honor to be, Sir,

Your obedient servant,

Signed William Tracy (?)

American Consul.

Fine Food Market.

By 1946 supermarkets outnumbered old-time Chinese merchandise stores, forty-five to nineteen. Stores with Chinese names such as Chung Kee, Kong Soon, Coon Chong Lung gave way to western names such as Grant Union, Best Food, Wonder Food, and H Street Market.

Best Food Market.

Wonder Food Market.

H Street Market.

CHAPTER EIGHT

From Mom and Pop
to Supermarts

Prior to the 1920s, Chinese retail food businesses were small stores that catered mainly to their own community. These were the businesses which took advantage of the exempt status of merchants under section six of the exclusion laws. From 1882 to 1913, the number of businesses in the Chinese quarter almost doubled from thirty-one to fifty-seven. However, by the 1920s, a new phenomenon in shopping began to take shape. Small mom and pop grocery stores began to expand their operations; men with entrepreneurial spirit pooled their resources together to cash-in on these new business ventures. The growth of supermarkets was noticeable. In 1921, the first of five Fulton Markets was opened at Fourth and M Streets. The grand opening of the Grant Union Market under Joe Yee added to the number of supermarkets under Chinese management.[1]

By 1946, supermarkets out numbered old-time Chinese merchandise stores forty-five to nineteen. Stores with Chinese names such as Chung Kee, Kong Soon, and Coon Chong Lung gave way to western names such as Grant Union, Best Food, Wonder Food, and H Street Markets. This was evidence of Chinese business acumen. These markets were located throughout the city and the target clientele was not just the Chinese community but the community at large.

In Sacramento, the Chinese were major innovators in the transformation of the typical practice of shopping daily at neighborhood grocery stores to purchasing groceries, produce, meat, fish, and poultry from a single large store. This was the concept of one-stop shopping convenience. Suburban sprawl established new residential districts, and the automobile contributed to the mobility of the population, promoting the rapid phenomenal growth of supermarkets following World War II.

Amazingly, without developed occupational skills, Chinese immigrants and native-born alike worked their way from domestic servants, cooks, and farm laborers to become leaders in the retail food industry. What is even more amazing, it began during the time when the nation was thrown into the worse economic depression of the century.

INDEPENDENT MARKET

Rose and Joseph Yee started their mom and pop store, the Independent, on the corner of Eleventh and Q Streets after their marriage in 1929. Rose's father was a cook for a "lo fon" (Caucasian) restaurant across the street from Chung Wah on Third Street between J and I Streets.

Joe Yee tried to expand his businesses by starting the Del Paso Market with Walter Fong. However, the partnership was not completed because of personal differences. Joe proceeded to open his own Grand Central on Sixth and G Streets, followed by Grant Union in 1936.

From Del Paso Market, Walter Fong also continued to expand his fledgling empire by opening Save-A-Lot and the Food Emporium. By 1949, he had established the Farmers Market chain, which at its peak had forty supermarkets.[2]

FULTON MARKET

One of the early supermarkets was Fulton Market, opened in 1921 on 400 M Street. The principals were Yee Noon Chung, his son Ging Yee, Yee Lim Chung, and Ned Chinn (aka Jew Tai Mork). Ned knew the meat trade as he had apprenticed with a German butcher. Noon Chung owned the Quong Cheung Lung store in Chinatown but invested in the market for his son. He remained a silent partner throughout the life of the business. In March 27, 1923, the partnership list consisted of nine active and eight silent members.

By 1937, they had a chain of five Fulton Markets; Fulton Quality Market at Sixth and M Streets; the Fulton Quality II at 918 J Street; the fourth store at Twenty-eighth and Broadway; and the fifth store Fulton Market Saving Center at Stockton Boulevard between Sixteenth and Seventeenth Avenues. However, as the nation headed towards World War II, the young men turned towards the defense industries and into the armed services, and the Fulton Market partnership dissolved. The business was taken over by Ging Yee's children. Ned Chinn started his own Ned Chinn Meat Company, which he operated at the Save-A-Lot Market.

(Courtesy of Florence J. Chinn, M.D.)

PARTNERSHIP LIST O

FULTON MARKET, 400 M street, Sacra
Filed by Jew Tai Mork, manager, in the c
12617/22751, and 22752 respectively, men

Jew Tai Mork,	manager,
Yee Chee,Shim,	buyer,
Yee Wo Ting,	salesman,
U. Khun,	salesman, (Vega
Yee Sang,	salesman,
Ong Dew,	salesman,
O Wai Chong,	salesman,
Wong Fun,	salesman & dri
Ong Fook Shee,	salesman,
Yee Noon Chung,	silent,
Yee Yea Chung,	silent,
Yee Chong Chung,	silent,
Yee Hein,Chung,	silent,
Yee Wui,	silent,
Choo Yee Wooi,	silent,	1000.00
Wong Kwong Fook,	silent,	1000.00
Wong Foo,	silent,	1000.00

Translated by

X. Fong.

Interpreter.

Jew Tai Mork Ong New Ong Fook Lee.
U Khun, Yee Lu Sim, Yee Wai Tung and
Lee Wu Chong were in the store March
27, 1923.

L.P. Hanson,
Inspector

FULTON MEAT MARKET
WHOLESALE & RETAIL
Phone Main 102-1111   400 M Street

Sacramento, Cal., _____ 192_

唐積本行多年人長股本一佰元

余志深買手占股車一佰元 外東余煖牛

余和情賣手占股車一佰元 余煖牛

余群賣手占股車一佰元 余昌中

余生賣手占股車一佰元 余顯中

鄧猷賣手占股車一佰元 余渭

歐維思賣手占股車一佰元 新其保

黃垣賣手占股車一佰元 黃光福

鄧福賜賣手占股車一佰元 黃密

雜祥三月廿年周環本業 每名占股壹佰元

Top row: Equal active partners

Yee Chee Shim (a.k.a.) Yim Lim Chung,
Yee Noon Chung and his son (a.k.a. Yee Wo
Ting) and Ned Chinn (a.k.a. Jew Tai Mork)
were principals.

Bottom row: Equal silent partners

GIANT FOODS

George Hong Quan came to the U.S. in 1919 along with Frank Fat, the future restaurateur. Both were sponsored by Dong Haw, proprietor of the Hong King Lum Restaurant. Years later, George Hong Quan, Chester Dong, Albert Dong and a few others opened the Liberty Meat Market on J Street off of Sixth Street. Liberty Market ran a successful business catering to the hundreds of blue collar workers at the Southern Pacific railroad shops and yard.

George's wife, Mary was ambitious and wasted no time starting work at the Del Monte Cannery. Using their savings, they then purchased a corner grocery store, the New Way Market. George Quan, Jr. was born in the living quarters behind the family store, New Way Market, on Sixth and P Streets where he grew up with his siblings, Richard, Gordon, and Betty.

During July 4th celebrations, the Quans also operated a sidewalk stall selling fireworks. When the city banned the sales of fireworks, the Quans went across the county line on I Street bridge to Broderick. There they rented part of a vacant store and continued their profitable fireworks sales. While in Broderick, they witnessed a small grocery store doing a high volume of business. Without hesitation they leased the vacant store that they were selling fireworks from, remodeled it, and opened their Eye Street Bridge Market, using proceeds from the sale of their New Way Market and their shares in the Liberty Meat Market. Not only were their customers from the Southern Pacific railroad yards and work shops, but they contracted to provide provisions for the agricultural labor camps along the Dixon, Knights Landing, and Davis corridor.

Wartime prosperity and the profitable years following provided an opportunity for expansion. The Quans opened a supermarket near McClellan Air Force Base, and then purchased Joe Yee's Grand Central on Fifty-ninth and Folsom, followed by opening the Giant Food Foothill. The stores were eventually consolidated under the operation of Giant Foods.

In the process of looking for sites for expansion, George Jr. recognized that opportunities in real estate investments were even better than the supermarket business. Currently on his desk in his home office are plans for the development of a high rise residential complex overlooking the Sacramento River.

Standing, left to right: George Woo, Mrs. George Hong Quan (Mary) Mary Lee. Children, left to right: Richard, Gordon, Betty, George Jr. (Courtesy of George Quan, Jr.)

Interior Eye St. Bridge Market
(Courtesy of George Quan, Jr.)

George Quan and wife Mary sold their New Way Market to open the Eye St. Bridge Market.
(Courtesy of George Quan, Jr.)

BEL AIR MARKETS

Yuen D. Wong came to California in 1868. After working in the mines, he returned to China to start a family. With prospects better in California, he returned with his fourteen-year-old son, Gin. Several years later, the two of them returned to China to arrange a marriage for Gin.

Gin returned to the United States in 1922. Five years later he brought his wife and five-year-old son to the United States. Gin was a sharecropper in the Loomis area until 1935. They eventually saved enough to purchase five acres in Penryn. Mrs. Wong grew vegetables and Gin sold the vegetables in Auburn door-to-door. Operations improved when they bought and converted a used truck into a mobile vegetable stand. Thus the Wongs raised six sons and a daughter in Penryn. One of their sons, Bill, gained experience working for grocery stores in Sacramento. In 1937, Bill went to Sacramento and worked for Walter Fong's Save-A-Lot on Sixteenth and F Streets and the Food Emporium store. After two years, Bill went to work for Harry Jan in his Fish and Meat Market.

Bill then went into business with Young Lee and purchased a store at Twenty-eighth and P Streets. Playing on the name of Walter Fong's store, Save-A-Lot, he named his store Save-More. The operation of the store was turned over to the family while Bill was in the service during World War II. Returning from the war, brother George located a new site which the family bought, and the first Bel Air Market was born. Inspiration for the name Bel Air came while the brothers passed through the Bel Air Estate district in Los Angeles County.

BENSON FONG

Benson Fong (the movie actor) worked at Save-A-Lot market with Bill Wong. On a double date they borrowed Walter Fong's a green International Harvester pick-up truck and drove all the way to San Francisco to Charlie Low's 365 nightclub. Agents from Paramount Studios were there scouting for Chinese actors. Films featuring battles with the enemy, the Japanese, were popular and Asian actors were needed. Ben went to Hollywood and thereafter was chosen to appear in many movies playing Japanese or any other Asian character, as needed.

The announcement of the opening of one of seventeen Bel Air supermarkets.

The teamwork among the family members sustained the business through good times and bad times, mistakes made and corrected. George, soft spoken and gentle, was the president. Bill assumed the arduous task purchasing produce twice a week during the wee hours of the morning from the San Francisco Produce Market, often at 2:00 a.m.; Albert and Lillie managed the meat department; Gene took care of finances; and Paul was in charge of building and truck maintenance.

The family marketing philosophy of quality and service coincided with their many innovative firsts, including the introduction of post office and banking services, childcare, and lending cold chests and coffee urns for picnics and parties to nonprofit organizations. In store No. 6, located in an area with a high concentration of Chinese people, they offered hot Chinese takeout food cooked in a wok in full view of their customers. Their five hundred employees were considered part of a big family. The Wongs shared their success with the Chinese community by giving generously—sponsoring golf tournaments, little league baseball, dinners, and charitable events.

By the time they sold to Raley's in 1992, they had a chain of seventeen supermarkets throughout the Sacramento area.

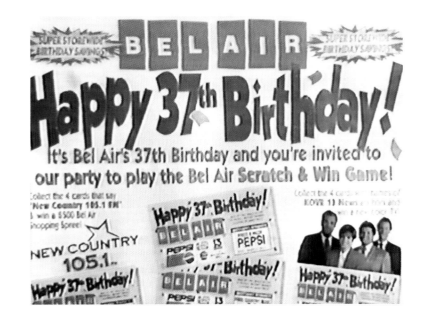

Dong Family 1921. Left to right: Sim, half-brother, Si-Chon, Liang Shee, baby Paul, cousin Eddie. (Courtesy of Paul Dong)

Registration of Liang Shee, merchant's wife. (Courtesy of Paul Dong)

To track the Chinese coming, leaving and returning to the United States, certificates of identity were mandated.

Registration of Si-Chon, merchant. (Courtesy of Paul Dong)

CHAPTER NINE

Wah Que and the Jook Sing

GUM SAAN HAAK

Chinese who immigrated to foreign lands are commonly called "wah que" (the overseas Chinese). Up until the early decades of the twentieth century, the Chinese population in America was predominately male. The wah que aspiration was to earn a living, as well as send a remittance home to support the family. His stay in the new land was intended to be temporary until he had amassed a modest fortune, enough to retire and live a life of leisure. His frugality, self sacrifice, and perseverance would be rewarded upon returning home. Visions of that moment of glory when returning with honor, prestige, and the envy of members of his hamlet sustained the reality of privation, living the lonely life of a bachelor. Upon his return to China, he would be anointed "Gum Saan Haak," (guest from the Gold Mountain).

Lok Wo, a distant relative of Yee Fung Chung, the herbalist, came to Sacramento during the gold rush. Lok Wo joined his uncle after the Exclusion Act of 1882, assuming the paper son identity of a native-born. Lok earned the nickname "Dai Pow Lok" (Big Gun Lok), not because he was a big shot but because he was always shooting off his big mouth! On a visit home, he brought with him mint rolls of shiny Indian head pennies. Playing his role as the struck-it-rich returnee, Gum Saan Haak, he would place a coin into the outstretched palm of each wide-eyed child of the hamlet telling him these were gold coins from Gold Mountain! After exhausting his modest savings, Lok returned to the United States to begin saving for a return trip. Lok died a pauper in the Stockton Hospital.

Amassing that pot of gold proved to be much more illusive, and took longer than most had anticipated. Some who were partners in a business could save enough and after a few years return home for a year or two. Single men would use the opportunity to secure a wife. After exhausting their earnings, they would return to the United States and toil a few more years. Some would leave their wife behind until their economic situation improved. During their stay at home, they would invariably register the birth of a baby boy for potential immigration.

Arriving on the same boat in 1919, George Hong Quan and Frank Fat became fast friends. Like most young men of the time, there was no time to be a teenager. They were already men, arriving penniless with a pocket full of dreams. Neither had any occupational skills so they took whatever jobs were available. George worked as a pastry and salad chef at the Land Hotel. Frank's jobs were less glamorous. He washed dishes at the Sutter Club, picked fruit in Isleton and Walnut Grove, and spent time in Cincinnati working in a restaurant. Eight years later they had managed to pay off the debts for their immigration, saved some money, and were ready to return home to choose brides. Although they came to the United States as young, unsophisticated, penniless country boys, both George and Frank now personified the cavalier, worldly, eligible, and desirable bachelors from Gum Saan. Typically the marriage was arranged by a matchmaker. The selected bride-to-be was the envy of the eligible maidens of the hamlet or village. Upon arriving to Gum Saan, the new wife discovered that the promises of Gold Mountain guaranteed nothing more than hard work. Nevertheless, the women of that era rose to the challenge, working alongside their husbands to raise families and through sacrifice, sending a modest sum home to support their families. The myth of Gold Mountain continued.

Nolan Lum's grandfather came to America several times and each time he would work a number of years to save about three hundred dollars and then return home to buy a piece of property. To the envy of his neighbors, with his frugal ways he managed to build a total of three houses in his home village. In 1920, Nolan's father, Lum Goon, was old enough to go to the United States. He purchased the birth identity of Lincoln Wong, the son of a citizen for four thousand dollars, through Wy Leong, an owner of the Far East Cafe in San Francisco. In preparation for the interrogation by immigration officials, Lum Goon memorized ten pages of "coaching papers," learning not only the family history of the paper father but the environment of the hamlet, description of the landscape, and the names of his neighbors.

FRANK FAT

After years laboring in Gum Saan, Frank Fat, George H. Quan, Bok Lung, Chester Dong and two other buddies eagerly booked passage for home to choose a bride. After weeks and weeks crossing the Pacific, the ship finally stopped over in Yokohama, Japan. The six excited young bachelors went ashore to see the town. They were having a great time when suddenly one of them realized, "Hey, we're going to miss the boat!" They rushed back to the pier just in time to see their ship sailing off in the distance. The option— take a motor launch to catch the ship. Each looked at the other with dismay as they reached into their empty pockets. The good time had cost them. All eyes turned to George, the well-known frugal one, who was still counting his money. George saved the day!

Frank Fat on his trip home to choose his bride, Yee Lai-Ching (Mary). Photo was taken in 1926 with his parents and family. Mary is third from the left, Frank holding baby Wing is third from right. (Courtesy of Chinese American Council of Sacramento)

The common experiences of hardship and survival bonded women together.

Lum (Mah) Lien Ung

Mrs. Ging Fong was among the hundreds of women who worked in the canneries during harvest time, ten hours a day, seven days a week, and still managed to raise a family. (Courtesy of Chinese American Council of Sacramento)

Mrs. Shee Fong at the center, surrounded by friends she made while working at the cannery. (Courtesy of Lana Chong)

Upon arrival in the United States, Lum Goon taught Chinese school in Locke during the evenings and worked on a fruit ranch by day. Earnings from working on the fruit ranch and teaching were too meager for survival, so he went to work for his sister's husband who was a partner in the grocery department of Save-A-Lot. After laboriously saving for thirteen years, Lum returned to China to find a wife.

Fifteen-year-old Mah Lien Ung lived in the hamlet of Gung Fah Chuen in Chung Shan. Traditionally, the hamlet had a list of eligible females and a matchmaker to arrange marriages. A Gum Saan Haak was always a preferred match. Lien proudly pointed out she was not from that list but was properly introduced to Lum Goon by a family member. He and Lien were married and had a baby boy. Lum was ready to return to the United States with his new family, but Lien Ung refused. The baby was born premature and was too frail to travel. For the sake of the baby's health, Lien Ung reluctantly urged Lum to return to the United States by himself. In 1949, Lum brought Lien Ung and his son, Nolan to the United States.

Paul Dong's father, Dong Sai Cheung, immigrated in 1899 as the paper son of Chin Si Chon. He worked at Sun Yee Yuen, a herb shop, and had a five hundred dollar investment to be a silent partner in the business. A community minded person, he was a board member of the Chung Wah School.

Dong Sai Cheung's wife died and in 1921, at the age of forty-six, he remarried and brought his young twenty-year-old wife Liang Shee back with him. Paul Dong said, "Mom was lucky to marry my Dad even though he was much older . . . to get away from all that poverty."

One generation later, Paul also returned to China to seek a bride. However, he didn't have to go through the humiliation of the immigration process that his father endured. Paul was a veteran of World War II and therefore qualified to bring Jeannie to the United States under the War Bride Act. As a teenager Jeannie had longed to marry a Gum Saan Haak so she could come to America. The opportunity arrived when her mother and Paul's mother, both working at a cannery in Sacramento, arranged the marriage.

Not everyone was so fortunate as to save enough money to make a trip home or to choose a bride. Desperately lonely and longing for home, some borrowed heavily and went into debt to make the journey. For everyone who managed one or more trips home, many more spent a lifetime in America, dreaming the same dream, never to make even one trip, never to see family and friends again. These were men with wives and children back home or single men who toiled from sunrise to sunset and sent their meager earnings back home. Men with little occupational skills, like the veteran of World War I, his name long forgotten, who was hired by a rancher to ride a horse day in and day out, up and down the field to chase birds away. It was affordable and more effective than using scarecrows. He died a pauper and was buried in the Chinese section of the City Cemetery, now in total disrepair.

For these unlucky men, home was in the basement below a store along I Street. A single twenty-five watt Edison clear bulb lit the passageway to their rooms. There were no windows for light or ventilation. Kerosene lamps lit their rooms. A few retreated to a room at the rear to toast a small portion of opium over an opium lamp and fill their pipes. Inhaling

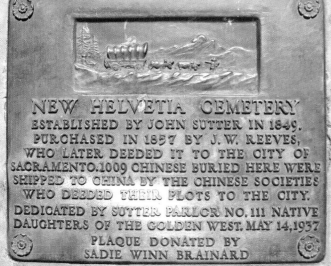

Plaque on the corner of J and Thirty-third Streets at Sutter Middle School.

For everyone who managed one or more trips home, many more spent a lifetime in America, dreaming the same dream, never to see family and friends again.

In the Chinese section of the City Cemetery is a grave stone marked Ah Wing, 1917. Could this be Ah Wing, the boxer, who died the same year? (Author's collection)

deeply, and oh so deeply, the American dream came in an opiate haze, and deep slumber.

The back rooms of the stores on I Street also served as living quarters for some families. Some stores were completely used for living when business failed. Dong Sai Cheung died at an early age and his family had to shut down the business. Daughter Margaret recalled the living conditions, "The living room was a storefront. There was no heat or hot water. We boiled water and put it into a large wooden vat for our baths, taken once a week, outdoors on the porch . . . We cooked on a small three-burner gas stove . . . there were three huge woks in the kitchen left over from the store . . . Because she worked . . . my mother frequently left us at home alone. She also taught me how to tell time so that 3:00 p.m. I was to turn on the cooking stove and start the rice . . . I was three . . ."

After their father's death, the family plunged into despair and poverty. The mother worked in the canneries and a local poultry shop to pay off debts and raise a family of seven. She worked at the canneries until a few months before her death at the age of sixty. Yet in her lifetime, she saved enough to buy a house.

It didn't take long to realize being the wife of a Gum Saan Haak also meant hard work. Both men and women, young and old, worked long hours, far surpassing the Protestant work ethic.

When George Hong Quan's wife, Mary first came to Sacramento, she worked both at the Del Monte Cannery, and with her husband at the Liberty Meat Market. Beef was purchased whole and delivered to the store in four quarters. Thereupon the butcher would break down each quarter into different parts. Each quarter weighed from 140 to 150 pounds; the hindquarter weighed from 80 to 100 pounds. Mary took on a man's job. With a quarter beef hanging from the rail, she could hold the beef with one hand and cut and saw with the other hand.

It was natural practice to buy live chickens and poultry to be slaughtered on site. Helen (Fong) Owyang slit the throats, drained the blood, and plucked the feathers of the chickens and ducks for customers of her father's Capitol Poultry Market. Nothing was wasted in the poultry business, and even the hot water used to defeather the chickens was collected by herb doctor, Henry Yee to cure patients with skin problems!

Although Chinese men first manned the canneries in the 1800s, by the 1900s the majority of the Chinese women worked in the canneries. Lien Ung worked for Del Monte. During harvest time, Del Monte hired about three hundred Chinese women, about two-thirds of them from Toishan. During the canning season, the women worked seven days a week, ten hours a day, at $1.25 an hour. Ninety-pound Lien Ung even took on the men's work of washing cans with a two-inch high pressure hose. Lien bragged, "I do four hundred cans an hour and four thousand cans a day. Washing cans was piecework." Said Lien, "I don't take toilet breaks!" The common experiences of hardship and survival bonded the women together. They shared moments of joy, such as the marriage of a son or daughter, or the one-month-old baby "red egg and ginger" party. While the canneries gave employment to many women in the twentieth century, it was the men in the nineteenth century whose labor initiated California's agricultural abundance that gave birth to the canneries.

The hope of returning home helped the sojourner sustain the life of bachelorhood and cushioned the constant alienation from the society at large. When the management of a vaudeville theatre on K Street refused to allow a group of Chinese to sit on the main floor, the Chinese called for a boycott of the theatre.[1] These incidents were reminders that anti-Chinese sentiments were alive and well. Aware of these prejudices, the Chinese in America made conscious efforts to promote and earn the goodwill of the public at large.

The Consul General Ho Yow in San Francisco initiated a general diplomatic policy to show the people of the United States the better side of the Chinese character, hoping to overcome prejudice. Following the establishment of an embassy in Washington, D.C., the Qing government assumed jurisdiction over the affairs of the overseas Chinese, the wah que. Opportunity came when committee organizers of the Sacramento Street Fair extended an invitation to the Consul General to sponsor a "Chinese Day." The Chinese accepted with enthusiasm. During Sacramento's Street Fair Week, on Wednesday, May 2, 1900, at 1:30 p.m., the Chinese showcased a parade the likes of which Sacramento had

(Courtesy of Dr. Doug Yee)

"Chinese Day" during Sacramento's Street Fair Week, May 2, 1900. "The skill of the Chinese pyrotechnical display is nothing short of miraculous . . . there is nothing ever seen in this country with which such a display can be compared." *Sacramento Bee* (Courtesy of Sacramento Archives and Museum Collection Center)

never seen before. The parade featured a spectacular three-hundred-foot long dragon, along with huge banners, cylindrical parasols, and glowing lanterns of every conceivable object and animal swaying in the breeze. The columnist of *The Sacramento Bee* wrote, "The skill of the Chinese pyrotechnical display is nothing short of miraculous" and regarding the Chinese parade, ". . . there is nothing ever seen in this country with which such a display can be compared."[2]

CULTURAL MAINTENANCE

In the era of exclusion, the wah que dominated and conducted the affairs of the community. Within their own social world, they built a network of organizations and institutions. In the early stages of settlement, the hui kuan, district associations organized by people from a common geographic location, were established to address the needs of the miners and protest unjust legislation. However, by the beginning of the twentieth century, the hui kuan in Sacramento had declined in influence. The Sam Yup hui kuan still existed in 1913, but the Yeong Wo, Sze Yup, and Ning Yeung founded in about 1854, had virtually disappeared from the scene.

The clan associations, bonded by their ancestral roots, continued to provide mutual aid and a place for socialization. Members with the same surname organized clan associations, purportedly descendants from a common ancestor famous in their clan history. Clan members with small numbers of surnames would form an association with multiple surnames.

Clan associations were usually extensions of the main headquarters first established in San Francisco. Only the Soo Yuen Benevo-

lent Association, representing the surnames Louie, Fong, and Kwong from the county of Hoi-ping (Kai-ping), established headquarters in 1859 on 416 C Street in Sacramento before it opened the chapter in San Francisco. The Lee immigrants organized the Lee On Dong Benevolent Association in the spring of 1880 on 401½ First Street; the Gee Tuck Sam Association, comprised of the surnames Wu, Cheu, Choy, Yang, and Tsao was organized in 1920 on 919 Third Street. The Yee Fung Toy represented the surname Yee. The Ong Ko Met Association, representing the surname Ong (also spelled as Dong, Deng, Tang, Tong, and Ung) was not established until 1942. According to oral tradition, the Wong Gong Hah Tong, representing the surname Wong, was established in 1875, but due to the lack of a home base, disbanded until it was reestablished in 1944 on J Street.

Whereas those organizations served the critical needs of the immigrants, the second generation found them archaic. Success in instilling the American-born youth with an appreciation for their ancestral roots was minimal. Assimilation into American culture was more a reality than embracing four thousand years of China's culture. Every clan association lamented its seemingly inevitable demise, and the dismal failure to attract the American-born generations of youths to continue the life of their associations.

Wing Kai Fat said his father, Frank was president of the Ong Family Association for one year. Kai concluded, "Why? Don't know how the association will survive. This generation doesn't need it, nothing for them. We are the last generation, who will take over? Not too many new Ong immigrants, most from Vietnam, Hong Kong, Taiwan."

Chinese community and students at the July 17, 1908, opening of Sacramento's first Chinese Language School (later renamed Chung Wah Chinese Language School), promoted by the Qing official Leung Hing Kuei. (Courtesy of Dorothy Y. Fong)

Nonetheless, community leaders continued to establish institutions within their own social world, including Chinese schools, in the hope that American-born generations would not forsake their cultural roots.

In 1908, the Qing government sent Commissioner Leung Hing Kuei (Liang Qinggui) to visit Chinese communities in the United States to promote knowledge and educate youth about their Chinese culture. Subsequent to his visit, a school named Que Lup Wah Gow Tong was housed at the Hin Jing Dong on I Street with an enrollment of twenty students.[3] The principal was Fong Jun Nom. The following year the school moved into the newly-established Chung Wah Hui Kuan on 915 Third Street. In 1931, funds were raised to build a new school at 522 Capitol Avenue, with the help of the Kuomintang and the theatrical group Teen Sing Seah.[4]

By this time the school (now renamed Chung Wah), the Confucian Church and the Chung Wah Hui Kuan became fused into one entity. That entity was incorporated under the name Confucius Church of Sacramento in 1935.[5] When the redevelopment agency of Sacramento bought the building, it built a new cultural center at Fourth and I Streets, which housed the school, the church, and the Chung Wah Hui Kuan. The building was dedicated on February 5, 1961. At that time, the Chung Wah Hui Kuan comprised Bing Kong Tong, Chungshan Memorial Hall, the Kuomintang, and the eight clan associations.

A number of immigrants (some of whom had been exposed to Christianity at home) were in the forefront of collaboration with the Protestant boards of foreign missions and societies not only in the propagation of the gospel but in instigating Chinese schools. Cultural maintenance was as important as embracing Christianity. The churches which taught a western religion and the schools which taught Chinese lessons, while seemingly contradictory, were inseparable. The American-born, while rejecting participation in the Chinese organizations, found common ground with their China-born parents in accepting Christianity.

Incorporating Chinese schools within the churches was one way to foster awareness of being Chinese. The earliest known school was the Chinese Baptist Mission in 1888 named Gee Yut Hawk How. In 1920, the Wah Yun Hawk How was established, followed by the Sun Do Hawk How in 1929, under the supervision of principal Chew Quan. The Kwai Wah School was founded in 1924 (affiliated with the Chinese Community Church). The Chinese United Methodist Church sponsored the Wah Mei School.

Right: Interior of Chung Wah School, circa 1940.
(Courtesy of Dr. Herbert Yee)

Below: Chung Wah School, 1939.
(Courtesy of Sacramento Archives and Museum Collection Center)

Kwai Wah Chinese School boys. (Courtesy Merrily Fong Wong)

"Went to Chinese school and learned to speak Sam Yup; at home we spoke Sze Yup; and in the day time we spoke English." —Audrey Fong Ah Tye

CANTON CHRISTIAN COLLEGE

The means of cultural maintenance included sending children to China to attend the schools founded by the missionaries. The Southern Baptist Church was headquartered in the Tung Shan district in Canton. The church founded two schools, Pui Ging for boys and Pui Do for girls. This neighborhood developed into a Christian community settled by the overseas Chinese. Children of college age were sent to the Canton Christian College, Ling Naam Hok Hau, which was initiated by the Presbyterian Mission in Canton. The campus is now Chung Shan University.

Among those who attended Ling Naam were Albert Hing and Howard Jan, both were distinguished athletes at the school. Jimmy Louie, whose family operated the Washington Meat Market, mentioned the existence of a chapter of the Ling Naam Alumni Association in Sacramento, of which he is a member.

Class of 1931. M. E. Church Chinese Language School.

YEE FUNG CHUNG FAMILY

At various times since 1898, five generations of the Yee Fung Chung family occupied J Street as their place of business and home. Yee Fung Chung named the business Yee Potai and Company, and ran the business with his son T. Wah Hing and two working partners, Yee Mow and Yee Sue. T. Wah Hing's daughters May and Rose were born here on the premises.

In 1906, returning home from a visit to China, T. Wah Hing brought with him his nine-year-old nephew, Henry Yee. Henry grew up at 707 J Street, and graduated from the University of Michigan with an engineering degree. He worked in Guangdong province and returned to Sacramento in 1929. Unable to find an engineering job due to discrimination, Henry followed in his grandfather's footsteps and became an herb doctor. For forty years, he practiced the Chinese art of healing at 707 J Street. Except for number four son Franklin, a medical doctor, Henry's oldest son Paul, and daughter May, both herbalists and chiropractors, Herbert and Calvin, both dentists, all practiced at 707 J Street. Herbert's sons Robert, Douglas and Wesley joined their father's practice and currently Wesley upholds the tradition practicing at 707 J Street.

Henry Yee and his wife Hum Wee Fong. Children left to right: May, Paul, Herbert, Song. (Courtesy of Dr. Franklin K. Yee)

(Courtesy of Dr. Franklin K. Yee)

T. Wah Hing and his family.
From left to right. Back row: Ella Yee, Rose Hing, Albert Hing, Viola Hing, Charles Hing Middle row: Gladys Yee, Donald Yee, #2 wife Laura with baby Virgil, T. Wah Hing, #1 wife Song Hing, May Hing, [she was missing on handwritten copy] Edmond Yee, Helen Hing
Front row: Ken Yee, Walter Yee, Richard Yee, David Hing, Eddy Hing(?), Edward Yee or Hing(?)
(Courtesy of Melvin Hing)

JOOK SING GENERATION

The wah que, confident and secure with their culture, had little need to accept the values of a foreign land. The American-born, however, were rapidly becoming acculturated. Disapproving elders admonished the younger generation for "been sigh lo fon" (turning into a white man) and derisively belittled the American-born as "jook sing" (referring to the plugged ends of the bamboo carrying pole).

Until the second half of the twentieth century, society at large looked upon all Chinese as foreigners, whether born in the United States or not. Interaction between the two societies was minimal at best. Dominated by provincialism within, American-born Chinese youths were still influenced by the values of mainstream America.

Real estate covenants kept the Chinese community from expanding from the confines of Chinatown. The neighborhood boundaries were within I and J Streets, and from Second to Eighth Streets, an area of some six blocks. Yet the community managed to persevere with its own social support system by creating their own social activities, worshipping in their own churches, and attending Chinese schools. Helen (Fong) Owyang said, "We visited each other's homes openly. We were secure among our own kind."

Cultural observances and the values of China, however, often still governed daily behavior. In particular, Chinese continued to celebrate the Chinese New Year, to make "joong" (sweet rice wrapped in bamboo leaves) for the festival of the fifth moon, and to celebrate the one-month-old birthday of a baby with a red egg and ginger party.

Problematic, however, was the social structure within the community. Prejudice existed even among the Chinese population. People from Sam Yup districts considered themselves superior to people from Sze Yup, with the Chung Shan people somewhere in the middle. Feisty ninety-year-old Rose Yee remembers her Sam Yup neighbor going to the temple to "bye son" (petition the gods) to break up the relationship between her number two son and a Sze Yup girl. Another neighbor was overtly hostile to the Sze Yup "doy" (boy) who dated her youngest daughter. On the other hand, Rose boasted, "She liked me even though I am a Sze Yup 'new-ee' (girl)." When Hing Owyang, Jr., a Heung Shan boy from Courtland, married Helen Fong, a Sze Yup girl and daughter of Chuck Fong and Lui Bik Chian, her parents were not happy. Hing said, "They resented me for years!" On the other hand, Helen said, "Mom said I'm getting old, better to be married than not."

To further complicate relationships, members of the same clan were considered related by common descent, and therefore forbidden to marry one another. A Fong could not marry another Fong even if there was no biological relationship. Even more absurd was the prohibition against marriage when the surnames were adopted through the non-biological relationship between paper father and paper son, which was used only to facilitate immigration. Socializing with other Chinese communities expanded the opportunities in finding a mate for American-born Chinese. Love was not to be denied, and many unions were formed despite the protest of outraged parents.

Besides dating, the interest of the second generation mirrored those of Anglo America in education, religion, entertainment, fashion, music and sports.

JOE N. YUKE FAMILY

Ruby Yuke's parents, Rachel Tso and Joe N. Yuke and her older siblings, from left to right: Howard, Anna, Andrew, and Daniel. Circa 1911–1912.

Ruby's grandfather came to Sacramento at the age of seventeen before the Exclusion Act and worked on the railroads. Her father Joe was born in Marysville, California. Joe worked for twenty-seven years as a cook for the Sacramento Sutter Club. (Courtesy of Ruby [Yuke] Fung)

Until the second half of the twentieth century, society at large looked upon all Chinese as foreigners, whether American-born or not.

SING FONG FAMILY

Mabel Tom's parents and siblings. From left to right. Back row: Edmund, mother May Dong Fong, father Sing Fong, Irving. Middle row: Jane, Mabel, Pauline, Eva, Amy. Front row: Edgar, Rose, Ruby, Edward

Mabel's mother was a Native-American and was raised by a Chinese Methodist minister in Boise, Idaho. Her father was an immigration interpreter.

(Courtesy of Ronald Tom)

NED CHINN FAMILY

Ned Chinn (Fulton Market) immigrated to Walnut Grove, California, in 1912 at the age of fifteen. He purchased the identity of a son of a citizen, Joe Goon Jay. By derivation, Ned became a citizen (albeit illegally). In 1918, he returned to China and married Leong See, the niece of Bing Lee, of the delta town Locke in California. Leong See did not join Ned until 1923, before the passage of the Immigration Act of 1924, which contained the provision that the alien wife of a Chinese-American citizen could not immigrate. (Courtesy of Florence J. Chinn, M.D.)

Ned and Leong See Chinn and their children, clockwise from left: Florence, Leland, Franklin, Gallant. 1930.

FONG SHEE FAMILY

Fong Shee (Quong Fang Co.) immigrated at age twenty. When he was twenty-seven, he returned to China to marry eighteen-year-old Wee Ping. Wee Ping joined her husband ten years later in 1936. Together, they raised eleven children. (Courtesy of Lana Chong)

From left to right. Back row: Carol, Rolland, Yvonne, Lorrie, Chris. Middle row: Joey, Lana, mother Wee Ping, Ron, father Fong Shee, Tom. Front row: Denny, Debbie.

FONG YUE PO FAMILY
Left to right: Wilma, Holland, Collin and Allen (seated), Marian, Virginia. (Courtesy of Virginia [Fong] Chan)

SAM FONG FAMILY—Wedding, June 15, 1947
Left to right: Ray Ah Tye, Audrey Fong Ah Tye, Edward Fong, Violet Fong Chan, Marie Mar Fong, William Fong, Yee Yee Fong, Sam Fong, Roger Fong. (Courtesy of Roger Fong)

CHAN TAI OY FAMILY

First row: Daniel Chan, Edward Chan, Thomas Chan, Violet Chong, Marjorie Chan, Dorothy Sun, George Chong, Davis Sun.

Second row: Grace Sun, Mrs. Chan Tai Oy (Lin), Wallace Chan, Mrs. Moy Sun, Grandma Chong, Mrs. Lee Chong (Lily), Edward Chong, Minnie Sun, Florence Sun.

Back row: Chan Tai Oy, Sun Kow, Lee Chong, Jue Chong, Sam Chong, Bing Chong, Look Chong.

(Courtesy of Dan Chan, Jr.)

Dan and Eddie, sons of Chan Tai Oy and Tung Lin Leong.

ENTERTAINMENT

Wayne Tom with David Sum, Gum Loc, Ed Chin, and Harry Wong formed a band, which toured the vaudeville circuit from California to Maine in the years 1927 through 1929. Appearing at the Earle Theatre in Atlantic City, a billboard advertised them as the "Musical Mandarins, China's Jazz Band." In Los Angeles they were featured at Solomon's Dancing Palace as "China's Greatest Jazz Band," even though all the members were born in America.

The Musical Mandarins. From left to right: David Sum, Ed Chin, Wayne Tom, Gum Lee, Harry Wong.

These young men toured and played in cities where the general public had never met nor set eyes on a "real" Chinese before. Watching this Chinese band play western music with western instruments was a novelty, and highly entertaining. Fortuitously, these early musicians were goodwill ambassadors, dispelling stereotypical imagery and promoting understanding, as well as bridging the gap of ignorance and intolerance.

WAYNE TOM

The band was playing in Chicago when Wayne saw his future wife, Mabel on a vaudeville stage featuring another Chinese group, Honorable Wu's Chinese Review on tour. It was love at first sight—Wayne was smitten by her beauty. The couple married and settled in Sacramento in 1931, where Mabel became very active in the Chinese Methodist Church. Wayne started a beer and wine distributorship. It was the era of the Big Bands when the music of Benny Goodman, Tommy Dorsey, and Glenn Miller swept the nation. Likewise in Sacramento, Wayne continued his passion for music by playing with his band in the evening at the Hong King Lum Restaurant and nightclub, popular with whites, and at the Lok Koon Restaurant on K Street.

Sisters Mabel and Amy Fong in Honorable Wu's Chinese Review. Wayne Tom saw the review and was smitten by Mabel's beauty. (Courtesy of Chinese American Council of Sacramento)

Boy Scouts of America Troop 14, Mee Wah School, 1931. (Courtesy of Chinese American Council of Sacramento)

American-born Chinese youths were still influenced by the values of mainstream America. Their interest in education, religion, entertainment, fashion, and sports mirrored that of Anglo America.

Sacramento Chinese Boys' Band, 1920. (Courtesy of Chinese American Council of Sacramento)

SPORTS

Baseball and basketball likewise were favorite activities among the youth. The earliest known baseball team was Chung Wah in 1912 with team members Chung Chan, Henry Yee, Ernest T. Yee, Arthur Wong, Bill Key Chan, Fred Kwong, Chancy Yee, Yen Fong, Gilbert Lee, and Charles King.

When Ed Chan's father visited Folsom Prison to negotiate for the release of a friend, the warden mentioned he had heard of the Chung Wah Chinese baseball team. He then invited them to play against the prison's team. The game was played on Thanksgiving Day in 1934. Ed Chan was the catcher, Ernest Yee was first baseman, Dan Chan outfielder, David Sum third baseman, and David Chan second baseman. Howard Jan played shortstop. Howard, manager and captain of the team, had gained the reputation of his peers as being good enough to play for the Sacramento Solons in the Pacific Coast League. The Folsom Prison team defeated Chung Wah. The score was too embarrassing to mention, but Ed Chan did confess it was in the double digits.

Besides the baseball team, Chung Wah also had a basketball team. These teams were organized for recreation and socializing. The team competed with other Chinese teams throughout the state.

Little known in the Chinese community was a former semipro basketball player, the late Wong Buck Hong, husband of Luceen C. Wong. He played for the Hong Wah Kue, the first and only Chinese semipro basketball team organized in San Francisco. The Hong Wah Kue played some one hundred games throughout Canada and the United States in the years 1939 to 1941. A reporter gave the team the supreme compliment when he wrote, "This will be the first time that the Harlem Globetrotters have played a team of their own caliber." Team members deliberately used their Chinese names for the sake of show biz. Wong Buck Hong's American name was Fred.

Like Wayne Tom's Musical Mandarins barnstorming America in the 1920s, the Hong Wah Kue's presence and performances promoted knowledge and goodwill for the majority of Americans who had never met a real Chinese person.

Chung Wah played against the Folsom Prison team on Thanksgiving Day in 1934. Chung Wah lost. The score was too embarrassing to mention, but Ed Chan confessed it was in the double digits. (Courtesy of Ella C. Fong)

Chung Wah School baseball team in 1912.
From left to right: Back row: Chung Chan, Henry Yee, Ernest Yee, Arthur Wong, Bill Key Chan. Front row: Fred Kong, Chancy Lee, Yen Fong, Gilbert Lee, Charles King. (Courtesy Ella C. Fong)

Chung Wah basketball team.
From left to right. Back row: Unknown, Edgar Fong, Ernest Yee, Howard Jan, Dave Jan, Howard Yee, Dan Yee. Front row: Richard Yee, Unknown, Unknown, Hank Fong, Eddie Chan, Harry Fong, George Chan. (Courtesy of Ella C. Fong)

The nineteenth century press had unmercifully emasculated the Chinese male. Any attempt by Chinese to engage in the manly and physical art of self-defense was ridiculed and made the butt of a joke. A notable exception was Ah Wing from Sacramento, who was described in the *San Francisco Chronicle* as the only Chinese professional boxer who was not only a clever boxer, but a hard hitter who possessed ". . . rare gameness."[6] Alas, upon reporting his death in 1919 the *San Francisco Examiner* couldn't refrain from the usual racial rhetoric, calling Wing the "little Chink" who made his debut with his flying queue and who "did not fail to create a sensation in the line of comedy." Some years later in 1920, another Sacramentan, bantamweight George Lee, fought a championship match in New Orleans. Though game, George lost the bout.[7]

After graduation from the University of California, Berkeley in 1933, John Jan went to work in the mining districts of California, Idaho, and Nevada. Encountering racism was to be expected anywhere, but especially away from the cities. One day working below ground, John was taunted by a crewmember. They went above ground to fight it out. The whole camp gathered to watch this 125-pound "Chinaman" who had dared to challenge a rough and burly miner much bigger than he. Eyes popped and jaws dropped in disbelief as everyone watched their fellow white miner be given a sound beating. Unbeknownst to him and his coworkers, John was the Pacific Coast featherweight champion in his collegiate days and had been a Golden Glove Champion.[8]

Ah Wing, Chinese Fighter

AMATEURS MEET THE YELLOW PERIL | CLOSE

AH WING WINS WITH PIVOTAL | **JIMMY BRITT IS SUFFERING SOME** | **WILL STAND FOR GRADUATE COACH**

Although described as a clever boxer, a hard hitter who possessed rare gameness, the newspaper could not resist poking fun of Ah Wing in this cartoon.

JOHN JAN

John Jan worked in the mining districts of California after graduation in 1933. Encountering racism was to be expected. Those who taunted John found out too late that he was the Pacific Coast intercollegiate featherweight champion.

(Author's collection)

The churches in the nineteenth century often conducted evening classes teaching English to entice the Chinese to follow the gospel. In a society consisting mostly of men focused on making a living, the progress of winning converts was slow. It wasn't until families and a second generation appeared that the Christian religion expanded and was seriously embraced.

By the dawn of the twentieth century, missionary activities intensified on both sides of the Pacific. In Canton, churches and schools were built to spread the gospel, and clinics and hospitals were built to spread the goodwill of the foreign religion. Every American town and city with a visible presence of the Chinese had its churches, missions, or institutions to indoctrinate the Chinese.

In Sacramento, Miss Eliza Willsie and Mrs. Mary Allen guided the Baptist Mission on 907 Fifth Street. The Methodist Chinese Mission on 919½ Third Street was under the leadership of Mrs. Marsh. Mrs. S. E. Carrington conducted evening classes at the Sacramento Chinese Church (Congregation Church) on I Street near Sixth Street, and Rev. A. J. Kerr came from San Francisco to deliver sermons at the Presbyterian Mission.[9]

Over the decades, transpacific missionary activities linked Christian communities on both sides of the ocean. After thirty-seven years in Shanghai and Hong Kong, Rev. Shuck returned and was appointed to Sacramento where he established the Chinese Baptist Chapel in 1854. After six years, Rev. Shuck retired and the American Baptist Home Mission Society sent women missionary workers to fill the void. In 1920, Rev. Yee Sur Wun was called from the Dong Shan Church in Canton. After a few years, he left for San Francisco, and in 1929, Rev. Lee Shau Yun, also from Canton, arrived to take his place.[10]

Immigrants who came under the influence of Christian schools in Canton reenforced the work of the Chinese missions when they arrived in America. Rachel Yuke, who attended the Mrs. Graves School established by Rev. R. H. Graves in Canton, taught Chinese school and Bible classes at the Baptist Mission in Sacramento.[11] Hiram Fong attended the Pearl River Academy in Canton, and upon arrival in Sacramento in 1917 at the age of twenty-two, joined the Chinese United Methodist Church at 915 Fifteenth Street.[12] He became the minister in 1924 and served for forty-three years until he retired at the age of seventy.

The Kwai Wah Chinese School, now the Chinese Community Church, RCA (Reformed Church in America) had an impressive enrollment. Immigrants Fong Sik, Chan Tai Oy, and Fong Bun Wall started the school by renting an old house on P Street between Fourth and Fifth in the spring of 1924.[13] Kwok Wei Sing from the Methodist Mission was engaged to be the teacher. No church was yet associated with the school.

In 1926, when the Chinese United Methodist Church started to build their new building, they lacked funds to complete the project. To help fund the building, the church negotiated to move the school into the new Methodist Church but when the church building was completed, the negotiations fell through. The Kwai Wah School purchased and remodeled an old house for their use on 519 N Street on December 13, 1926, and named it the Chinese Christian Church with Kwok

Dongshan Church in Canton.
Philip Choy, the author, visited China in 2006. On a Sunday morning, he was in the Dongshan district in Canton to inquire if there was ever a church there. He recollects, "Walking up a street I was amazed to hear singing of church hymns. An elderly woman saw my startled expression and exclaimed, 'Bye Yeah So!' (worshipping Jesus). I followed the music and behold! In front of me was the church where Rev. Yee Suey Won was pastor before he came to Sacramento to be the pastor of the Chinese Baptist Mission in 1920." (Author's collection)

Baptist Mission.
Back row: Mrs. Mary Allen, second from left wearing a hat. Middle row, second from left to right: Mrs. Dong Haw, Florence Sun, Anna Yuke, Ruby Yuke, Grace Chun, unknown, Rose Abe. Front row, left to right: Rose Dong, Bill Dong, Richard Dong, Hattie Chun, Donald Chun, Lily Dong, Jerry Dong, Stephen Lee, Helen Yee (Courtesy of Ella C. Fong)

Wei Sing conducting religious services.[14] Kwok Wei Sing was not actually a minister, so on August 16, 1931, the Chinese Christian Union in San Francisco held a ceremony at the Chinese Presbyterian Church and officially ordained Kwok Wei Sing.

While the thrust of missionaries was toward winning converts, conversion to Christianity for the Chinese was a step toward assimilation. Assimilation, however, did not guarantee integration. Chinese continued to worship in segregated churches labeled as missions.

Until World War II, most Americans had never come into contact with a Chinese person. The churches, like Wayne Tom and the Musical Mandarins and Fred Wong with the Hong Wah Kue baseketball team, introduced the Chinese to mainstream America.

Their national newsletters carried news and progress of converting the Chinese. A lantern slide show, entitled Understanding the Oriental Americans was made in the early 1930s by the Methodist Episcopal Church to introduce the public to the Chinese who lived in America. The lecture pointed out, "Many people in America have never seen a Chinese child . . . they speak English . . . much more . . . than the language of their parents . . . they are far more American than Chinese."[15]

While transpacific evangelistic activities continued among the Chinese, mainstream America cared less. As long as the Chinese kept to themselves, most evidence of prejudice remained covert. It was outside the community that verbal and physical prejudice was encountered.

Kwai Wah Chinese School, 1931. (Courtesy of Dan Chan, Jr.)

Kwai Wah circa 1947. (Courtesy of Sacramento Archives and Museum Collection Center)

M. E. Church ministers, 1931.

M. E. Church members. Hiram Fong was the minister. (Courtesy of Dr. Douglas Yee)

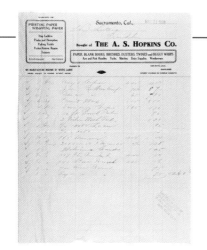

Anti-Chinese sentiments prevailed at the turn of the 20th century. Note the phrase "We manufacture brooms by white labor" on the letterhead. (Author's collection)

AGAINST ALL ODDS

Ninety-year-old Rose Yee proudly recalled her days in 1936 when she and husband Joe operated the Independent Market which served mainly Caucasian customers. Rose quipped, "you have to take a lot in those days. You have to be one jump ahead." One white customer called her "Chinaman" and "hatchetman" every time he came into the store. Rose had had enough and the next time he came in she told him off. "I'm proud I'm a 'Chinaman.' I can count my ancestors back three or four thousand years. Can you?" The customer turned red and never came back.

During World War II, food was rationed and purchases had to be accompanied by ration stamps. Often white customers would try to cheat her by asking her to cut a portion of meat and cheese larger than the stamps they had. She got wise and began asking for the stamps first. One white customer was offended and berated her by saying, "You damn Chinamen! If it weren't for you we wouldn't have this war!" Rose ignored him and proceeded to wait on others. The customer demanded, "Are you going to wait on me?" Rose snapped back, "We're not good enough for you . . . you go to where they are good enough for you to get what you want."

Maintaining her pride and dignity were more important than keeping a customer. These bigoted attitudes prevailed until World War II.

Ostracized by social clubs, banned from certain employment opportunities, and limited by real estate restrictions, the Chinese did not share in the benefits of Sacramento's growth and wealth that they helped to produce. It was clear the Chinese were not intended to be a part of America. The rejection in America was a direct reflection of the weakness of the decaying Chinese empire. The Chinese who left Guangdong in the nineteenth century did not possess any interest in the politics of the Manchu government and had little concept or consciousness of nationalism and loyalty to the government. The overseas Chinese in twentieth century America looked forward to a future when China would unify and rise up to overcome the destructive forces that undermined her sovereignty. Opportunity came when parties with opposing ideologies arose to salvage China, by inspiring nationalism among the overseas Chinese. This was further enhanced by the fact that both leaders of the opposing parties were from the province of Guangdong. Even those of the second generation, feeling disenfranchised from America, adopted the fervor of patriotism towards China.

From left to right: Back row: Walter Fong, Hal Yee, Gordon Fong, Gerald "Nipper" Fong.
Front row: Jimmie Yee, Joseph Fong, William Fong, Robin Gee, Fee Min Louie. (Courtesy of Fee Min Louie)

Roger Fong remembers: "Chinese sports and social youth clubs during the 40's formed because of discrimination, like the Wah Yen (Chinese boys club), who had an annual dance called 'Blossom Time,' carnivals to raise funds, and usually a very good basketball team that played other Chinese teams from out of town like SF, Stockton, etc. All done without adult sponsors. The Black Panthers was a football team made up of Sacramento and Delta boys. Another was the Marauders, a men's baseball team. Girls clubs such as the Wah Lung, The DeMoi's (play on sisters in Chinese), a girls' sorority formed because the white clubs did not accept Asians. All of these groups formed prior to our gradual assimilation into high school and college sports and clubs in the '50s."

The team could not afford warm-up suits so they wore matching pajamas. (Courtesy of Fee Min Louie)

HOMELAND POLITICS

Until 1949, the majority of emigrants came from the Province of Guangdong. Leader of the reform party Kang Yu-wei, and his opponent Dr. Sun Yat-sen, leader of the revolutionary party, were both from Guangdong, and recognized the importance of the overseas Chinese as their support. Kang, a native of Nomhoi and an intellectual of the Confucian school, advocated solving China's problems by reform. He looked to the wealthy merchants for their support. Sun, a native of Heung Shan, advocated overthrowing the monarchy and establishing a republic. He appealed to the working class of laborers, small shopkeepers, and laundry workers. Ultimately, it was Dr. Sun's revolutionary party that gained the confidence and support from the overseas Chinese in America.

A chapter of the Chinese Empire Reform Association was founded in Sacramento in 1904. Note that some of the members have abandoned traditional Chinese dress. (Courtesy of Anna Wong Lee, Sacramento Archives and Museum Collection Center)

(Courtesy of Chinese American Council of Sacramento)

Sun's early collaborator was Lu Hao Tung, who came from his home village of Cuixiangcun. The two of them had similar exposure to western culture, in particular to Christianity. Sun received his Christian education at the Iolani College in Hawaii. Hao Tung's father had a business in Shanghai where Hao acquired facility in English, and he too became a Christian. When his father died, Hao returned to Cuixiang at about the same time Sun, now age sixteen, returned to Choy Hung from Hawaii.

In the years 1886–1887, Sun attended the new foreign missionary Canton Hospital School, which Hao Tung also attended. The two young men roomed together and spent hours talking passionately about overthrowing the Manchu monarchy. Meanwhile Sun attended the Alice Memorial Hospital School (1887–1892) and after graduation, Sun set up a medical practice in Macao. His medical practice, in addition to providing a livelihood, disguised his activities of recruiting followers for his cause. For six months Sun and his fellow conspirators laid plans to attack the provincial government in Canton. They began clandestinely purchasing and shipping arms and ammunition to their headquarters in Canton. The plot was discovered and the headquarters was raided. Everyone escaped including Sun. However, Hao Tung returned to retrieve the membership list and was caught. Hao was tortured with bamboo slivers driven under his fingernails and toenails in an attempt to coerce him to reveal the names of the conspirators. Hao heroically refused, and on November 7, 1895, at the age of twenty-seven, Hao was executed, the first martyr to die for the revolution.

LU HAO TUNG

Descendants of Lu Hao Tung made Sacramento their home. Hao Tung's granddaughter, Rose Luke, stunned the Chinese community with her beauty when she arrived in Sacramento as the bride of Chan Tai Young (aka Carl Y. Chan), a member of the business firm Tong Sung. She became known as Dai Yut Le-ang (number one beauty) of Chinatown.

Grandson Quan Luke came to Sacramento in 1941, just before Japan attacked Pearl Harbor. The Kuomintang government, recognizing he was the descendant of Hao Tung, allotted him five thousand dollars for schooling in the United States. After the United States entered the war, Quan joined the armed forces. The remaining members of the family came after World War II to escape the ravages of war. Ching So Ping, daughter-in-law of Hao Tung, and her children Jane, Leung, Elton, and Calvin all came to Sacramento. The great granddaughter of Lu Hao Tung is Florence Fong, wife of Roger Fong.

Rose Luke-Chan
(Courtesy of Florence Fong)

In the summer of 1909, the members of Dr. Sun's revolutionary party from San Francisco, led by Wong Won So and Wong Bok Yu, went to Sacramento to organize a chapter of the Tung Meng Hui.[16] Attending the meeting, held at the Fourth Street dental office of Leong Teen Min, were some twenty followers, mainly working class youths who were eager to take the oath and ready to be sworn in.[17] The ceremony took place at the Leet Sing Gung Temple at 915½ Third Street (later the location of the Chinese Benevolent Association), officiated by Wong Won So. Wong Jurn Sam was elected chairperson and one half of the store at 404 I Street where Fong Woon Duk lived was designated a place to hold weekly meetings.

When Dr. Sun arrived, he stayed and spoke at the Chee Kung Tong, a secret society once dedicated to the overthrow of the Ching dynasty and to restore the Ming dynasty. He then met with Wong Jurn Sam, Fong Chuck, Fong Yue Po, Fong Ming Sun, Fong Lum, and Fong Woon Duk at the Suey Sing tailor shop at 611 J Street to discuss the revolution and to sew the party flag; a twelve pointed white star against a dark blue background, designed by the martyr Lu Hao Tung. Fong Chuck remembered the occasion and said of Dr. Sun, "He was friendly and jovial."

Following the revolution of October 10, 1911, five members of the party returned to take positions in Dr. Sun's government in the new Republic of China. They served as Dr. Sun's bodyguards.

Following the revolution of 1911, five members left Sacramento to join Dr. Sun Yat-sen's Nanking government. Back row, position from left: (#1) Gum Wah Ying, (#4) Fong Chuck, (#5) Fong Woon Duk. Front row, position from left: (#1) Fong Lum, (#2) Wong Bo Sahm. (Courtesy of Helen Fong Owyang)

Fong Yue Po, founder of Lincoln Market.

Fong Yue Po, his brother Fong Ming, and Fong Chuck personified the patriotic fervor of their generation.

Fong Ming

Fong Chuck was one of the five men from Sacramento who returned to China to serve as Dr. Sun Yat-sen's bodyguard. (Courtesy of Helen Fong Owyang)

Fong Chuck came to Sacramento at the age of eighteen from Toishan. He immediately immersed himself into the ideology of the revolution and joined in its activities. Upon his return to Sacramento from China, he continued his patriotic efforts and served as President in the Sacramento chapter of the Kuomintang (KMT), the political party of the Republic of China after the revolution. Later he was Vice President of the *Young China* newspaper in San Francisco. He also participated in affairs in the community as Chairman of the Board of the Chung Wah School for twenty-nine years, and in the 1960 redevelopment planning of the new Chinatown. After working at a restaurant at 209 K Street, then at the poultry and fish department of Lincoln Market at 318 I Street owned by fellow patriot Fong Yue Po, Fong Chuck started Capitol Poultry and Fish Market.

Fong Yue Po's older brother, Fong Ming was the first of four brothers to come to the United States. He taught at Chung Wah Chinese School in 1917 for a few years and then became editor in chief of the *Young China* daily newspaper in San Francisco.

Fong Yue Po, Fong Chuck, Gum Wah Ying, Fong Lum, and others personified the patriotic fervor of their generation at the turn of the century when China was under the inept and corrupt rule of the Manchu monarchy and under the pressures of foreign imperialism. Japan's aggressive attempts to occupy China forged a spirit of nationalism and unity never before seen in the community in which the wah que and the American-born men and women rallied together to defeat Japan.

In a December 2, 1973 article in the *Sacramento Union*, renowned herb doctor Henry Yee exclaimed, *"In those days, all Chinese wanted to go back and help build their country."* Henry did. After graduating from the University of Michigan, he worked for the Michigan Department of Highways. On October 28, 1924, he sailed for China and was Chief Engineer for the Swatow Canton Railroad. After five years, he returned to Sacramento. The year 1929 was the time of the Depression and discrimination was still prevalent. Unable to find employment, he gave up engineering and took up his grandfather Yee Fung Chung's occupation as an herb doctor.

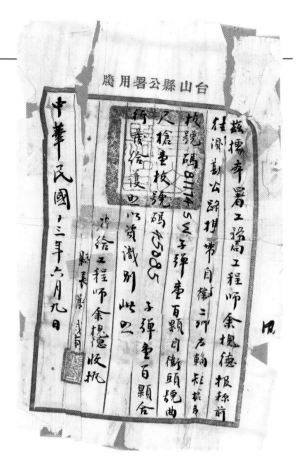

This gun permit was issued in 1924 by the Toishan government to Henry while he was working in Guangdong. (Courtesy of Dr. Franklin K. Yee)

Mr. K. L. Fong, president of the Young China Newspaper, participating in the Dragon Dance.

An elaborately decorated float in the parade.

One novel approach to raising funds was a three night event called China Night. (Author's collection)

When Ned Chinn (Fulton Markets) was a young boy of fourteen in China, he dared to cut off his queue, the symbol of subjugation under the Manchu rule. Ned carried this spirit of activism into his adulthood as he engaged in political activities in Sacramento dedicated to the salvation of China. He joined and became active in the KMT.

Ned was chosen Chairperson of the Sacramento Chapter of the National Salvation League during the year 1937, to raise money for the casualties of the war. Actively engaged and serving in committees were old timers Fong Yue Po and Fong Chuck, along with leaders of the New Life Movement, Mrs. Irene Fong, Vice President, and Mrs. Doris Leong. The organization promoted bonds for all members of the community in denominations of ten dollars to fifty dollars. However, the sale of bonds was determined to be a violation of United States Government regulations. Thereafter volunteer donations were solicited instead.

Whereas the spirit of patriotism existed among the majority of the overseas Chinese, a few were not so enthusiastic when it came to buying bonds issued by the National Salvation League to support the war effort. Every Chinese in America was expected to display their patriotism by sacrificing their income to the maximum. The minimum bond of ten dollars in 1937, and of fifty dollars in 1940, was a financial burden for those earning a dollar a day, which is what many seasonal laborers were paid.

One novel approach to raising funds was a three-night event called China Night. The gala affair was a display of patriotic fervor. Three nights of continuous patriotic plays,

movies, dancing acts, choral and solo singing, and Chinese opera energized the Chinese community with national fervor for China. Weeks and weeks before the event, the student body of every Chinese school and church was busy planning and practicing in preparation. Mabel Tom, a prominent figure in the Methodist Episcopal Church, and Rose Fong directed a fashion show. Ann Jan, a leader in the Baptist church, directed the Mee Wah students in a medley of Chinese anthems opening with Beautiful China. Likewise, Rachel Yuke led the Chung Wah students and W. S. Kwok directed the Kwai Wah students.

All members of families—young and old, men and women—participated in the fight for the salvation of China. Patriotism towards the homeland bonded the first generation with the second generation. Discussions on the sovereignty of China were held among youths. Most talked the good talk, but a few like John Jan, walked the walk.

John grew up in Sacramento. His father established Wing Lee Meat Market in 1913. His mother was a member of the women's group, New Life Movement.

After earning a degree in mining engineering and following his work in the mining districts of California, Idaho, and Nevada, he decided he was ready to join in the "salvation of China" in the struggle against Japan. On August 9, 1940, he sailed for Hong Kong. Fortuitously, he met Rewi Alley, the renowned New Zealander who, with Edgar Snow, was instrumental in founding the Chinese Industrial Cooperatives, also known as Indusco. The C.I.C. program was to mobilize the scattered labor and disrupted production in war-torn China, and to build industrial bases to sustain China's battle for

Patriotism toward the homeland bonded the first generation with the second generation.

Gen. Tsai Tin Kai, from Kaiping, Guangdong, won the hearts of the overseas Chinese as a national hero who led his 19th Route Army into battle against the Japanese in Shanghai, defying orders from Chiang Kai Shek to retreat. In his visit to America, the Chinese communities celebrated his presence with patriotic hysteria and feted him with ovations, banquets, and parades. (Author's collection)

Chinese community and students at the 1908 opening of Sacramento's first Chinese Language School (later renamed Chung Wah Chinese Language School), promoted by the Qing official Leung Hing Kuei. (Courtesy of Chinese American Council of Sacramento)

Chung Wah and Kwai Wah School Drum Corp ready for the parade honoring General Tsai Ting Kai, 1935. (Courtesy of Chinese American Council of Sacramento)

Women's New Life Movement. Women were equally dedicated to a unified China. (Courtesy of Virginia F. Chan)

survival against Japan. Upon discovering that John was a mining engineer, Alley immediately hired him and together they left for the southeast headquarters of the C.I.C. at Kan Hsien, Kiangsi.

For nine years John crisscrossed free China (unoccupied by Japan) by boat, bus, or truck, and most of the time by foot, walking as many as thirty kilometers a day. With his head shaven and wearing grass sandals, his sleeping bag for a bed, he logged thousands of miles. Often his meals consisted of only two black beans and sauce to scoop down his bowl of rice. His starting salary was nine dollars a month. His assignment—to investigate the mining, industrial, and technical conditions in the southeast region.

After four years with C.I.C., John left, and worked for the United Nations Relief and Rehabilitation Administration (UNRRA) as an industrial rehabilitation field officer of coal mining in Shanghai. During this period he took interest in a young woman Joanne, and they were married in 1946.

The Allies defeated Japan, but the glory of victory was clouded by the ominous shadow of civil war between the Communists and the KMT. John and his wife returned to Sacramento in 1948.

John became active in the civil rights movement of the 1960s and 1970s, and the normalization of relations between the U.S. and China. During this period, the vision of his youth for a strong China was rekindled. In his continuing correspondence with Rewi Alley, the two old timers reminisced about old times and romanticized reviving the C.I.C as still viable for the industrialization of the People's Republic of China. At age seventy-three, John was making plans to return to China. This was not to be, as he died of cancer in 1983.

The display of patriotism caught the attention of a sympathetic America. Negative attitudes took a positive turn for the Chinese in America when Japan attacked Pearl Harbor on December 7, 1941. Suddenly, the Chinese were thrust into mainstream America. It took the widespread enmity against a new nemesis, the Japanese, to accomplish this.

PART V

BRIDGING THE GAP

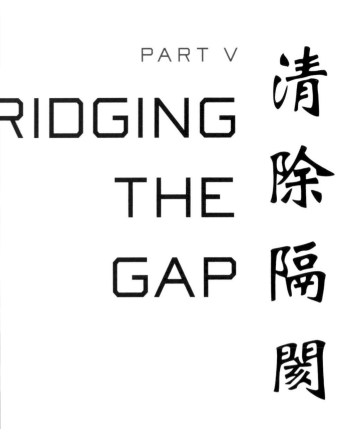

清除隔閡

World War II was clearly the turning point for socio-economic improvements for the Chinese.

TELEPHONE
CLASSIFIED ADS TO
SUtter 2424
(East Bay, TEmplebar 2420)
or bring them to
Examiner Office
Corner Market and Third Sts

AN AMERICAN PAPER · AMERICA FIRST · AMERICAN PEOPLE

San Francisco Examiner
Monarch of the Dailies

VOL. CLXXV, NO. 161   CCCC★ ★★★★   SAN FRANCISCO, MONDAY, DECEMBER 8, 1941—32 PAGES   DAILY 5 CENTS, SUNDAY 10 CENTS PER MON.

3,000 HAWAII CASUALTIES

Parachutists Invade Philippine
Thailand Yields to Japanes

IN THE NEWS

WELL, fellow Americans, we are in the war and we have got to win it.

There may have been some difference of opinion among good Americans about getting into the war, but there is no difference about how we should come out of it.

We must come out victorious and with the largest V in the alphabet.

We are not completely prepared for war.

We may not have got a Swiss system of universal service that we will have to have some day, since the lands are full of robbers and sea of pirates.

But we will get better and stronger every day, and we will not have to get very good and very strong to knock the everlasting daylights out of Japan.

We may have some small reverses at first, but do not let that worry you—if it happens.

It is not who wins the first round but who wins the last one that counts for victory.

And there is no doubt about the victory, folks—none whatever.

The worst thing about the war with Japan is that it will divide our efforts and prevent us from rendering the all out aid to England that we are pledged to give.

Nearly 1,500 Dead In Honolulu Raid, Many Planes Lost

By The Associated Press.

WASHINGTON, Dec. 8 (Monday).—The White House announced today that the Japanese attack on Hawaii had resulted in the capsizing of an old battleship, the destruction of a destroyer, damage to other vessels and destruction of a relatively large number of planes.

It added that several Japanese planes and submarines had been accounted for.

An official White House statement, the first authentic Government appraisal of the attack yesterday, said that casualties were expected to mount to about 3,000, nearly half of them fatalities.

More Planes Rushed to Islands

It was disclosed that active resistance was "still continuing" against the Japanese attacking force in the vicinity of Hawaii. Re-enforcements of planes are being rushed to the islands the White House said, and repair work is under way on ships, planes and ground facilities.

The White House said that Wake and Midway Islands, in addition to the Island of Guam and Hong Kong, China, had been attacked but that details were lacking.

Asked whether there was any official information why Japan was able to get inside the outer defenses of the Hawaiian group, Presidential Secretary Stephen Early said it was the consensus of experts that probably all the attacking planes came from carriers which had moved forward during the night and sent their planes aloft. The attack came at dawn yesterday.

There was no identification of the battleship which capsized beyond the statement that she was an old one. The ship turned over in Pearl Harbor, the Navy's giant Hawaiian base.

Other Ships Badly Damaged

The statement said that several other ships "have been

S.F. Rounds Up Japs, Swings to Defense

A roundup of Japanese aliens in San Francisco and other West Coast cities was in progress last night.

Squads of Federal Bureau of Investigation agents and police ranged through San Francisco's Japanese section, taking into custody undisclosed numbers of "suspicious aliens" considered as potential saboteurs.

Meanwhile San Francisco swung swiftly to a war footing with these things happening:

1—The Army and Navy, cancelling all leaves, manned San Francisco's shore, air and sea defenses on a twenty-four hour basis. (Details Page 10.)

2—The Navy took command of all shipping in San Francisco Harbor and notified companies that all commercial ship movements henceforth must be under Navy command. (Details Page 10).

3—The Army Air Force put its raid warning service in instant operation, trimmed its interceptor planes for instant action and took over all antiaircraft artillery from the Fourth Army command. (Details Page 10).

4—Guards were flung around strategic bridges, defense plants, water supplies, railroad tunnels and other points—all under direction of Maj. Gen. Jay L. Benedict, commanding general of the Ninth Corps Area. (Details Page 10).

5—Mayor Rossi proclaimed a state of emergency, a step which under the city charter

(Continued on Page 10, Col. 1)

BULLETINS

BANGKOK (Thailand), Dec. 8.—(AP)—Thailand, after brief resistance to Japanese invasion from the sea and across the French Indo-China border, ceased firing today and opened negotiations with the invaders.

The results of the negotiations were expected to be announced shortly.

(In Tokio the Board of Information said an agreemnet was reached to permit passage of Japanese troops through Thailand.)

Japanese forces poured into Thailand from three coastal points, Prachuapgirikhand, Singora and Patani, which are on the southernmost part of Thailand's Gulf of Siam coast, close to British Malaya, and across the land frontier from their southern Indo-China base at Siebreap.

(Domei broadcast from Tokyo that the Japanese Embassy in Bangkok reported that British forces had crossed from Malaya into Thailand shortly after dawn this morning and were being swept back by the Japanese. Japan, it said, was acting to save Thailand's independence and peace.

(CBS in New York heard a British broadcast quoting official British advices that the Japanese are in possession of southern Thailand.)

There are about 200 United States citizens in Thailand. Those in the north were advised to remain temporary where they are and try soon to leave by way of Burma.

The American legation here has invited United States citizens to go to it.

TOKIO, Dec. 8 (Monday).—(AP)—The navy section of the Imperial headquarters announced today two American battleships were sunk, four others damaged and four heavy cruisers damaged at Pearl Harbor by Japanese naval bombers during the attack yesterday.

The naval statement, broadcast on the Tokio radio, said there were no Japanese losses.

Imperial headquarters also declared that a United States aircraft carrier was sunk by a submarine off Honolulu.

It said Japanese planes which attacked Guam early today were reported without confirmation to have sunk the 840 ton minesweeper Penguin.

The headquarters announcement said many merchant ships had been captured in the Pacific and declared there was no indication that any Japanese ships had been lost in the day's operations.

Honolulu Bomb Twice; Hundre Die; Warships

NEW YORK, Dec. 8 (Monday) —Royal Arch Gunnison, in a broadc Manila, reported today that Japane chute troops had been landed in the pines.

He said native Japanese had control of some communities whe are thickly concentrated, but said other sections Filipino police were ro up Japanese Nationals and taking concentration camps.

Gunnison also reported, withou that "in the naval war the ABCD under American command appeare successful against Japanese air a invasions."

By The Associated Press.

Japanese warplanes made a deadly a Honolulu and Pearl Harbor Sunday in the of a series of surprise attacks against Amer British possessions throughout the Pacific pore and the Malay Peninsula were attacked and air.

Three hours later the Japanese Govern clared war on the United States and Great

Soon a second wave of Japanese bombers shocked Honolulu.

News that the second attack was just sta phoned to President Roosevelt by Governor Poi Hawaii at 2:30 p.m., Pacific time. Censorship pr and no direct word from Hawaii reached the main that to tell what damage had been done in the se or what retaliation had been visited on the invaders Governor Poindexter told the President, th

CHAPTER TEN

World War II—the Pivotal Point

When Japan attacked Pearl Harbor on December 7, 1941, never in the history of the United States was there such an upheaval of the masses as the whole nation mobilized for war. Patriotism bonded people of different colors and of different backgrounds together. Patriotism also blinded us from justice as fellow Americans were branded the enemy because they were born of Japanese descent.

China was now an ally of the United States. Therefore, the Chinese in America were comrades in arms with mainstream America. Men and women of all colors worked in the defense industries. Every family who had sons of age sent those sons into military service. Patriotic fervor was such that in some families, multiple boys were in the service, like Joe Wayne Fong and his three brothers. Another example was Tim Jang and his four brothers, Edwin, Edward, Edgar, and Joe were in the service; in addition, their sister, Winnie joined the WAC.

Joe Wayne Fong saw action with the 773rd Tank Destroyer Battalion 90th Infantry Division. Joe wrote, "My experience in the war is somewhat difficult to fathom. People and animals getting killed, towns and buildings destroyed, people under extreme hardship and many innocent people displaced. I thank the superior being for watching over us."

William (Wai Yee) Fong served in the Defense Department of the Army. He was a member with six others who were designated electronic communication experts. In preparation for the attack on the Anzio Beachhead, General George Patton and his staff met with the team to resolve communications between tanks. When asked how he intended to command his tanks, the General gruffly stated, "This is a suicide mission! We don't command, we just go!"

In wartime civil service, private industries and businesses lowered their barriers toward employment of the Chinese. More important than discrimination was the desperate need for manpower in the defense industries.

William Fong's father, Fong Wing Puy, and uncle, Fong Wing Fook, immigrated and went to Blue Canyon to take over their father's store next to the railroad station. They later moved to Sacramento in order to provide a better environment to raise a family. Wing Fook opened the Superior Market at 930 Q Street where Wing Puy worked as the bookkeeper. In order to support his family of four, he also worked at the Senator Hotel in charge of the pantry until World War II when other employment opportunities opened up. No longer having to work two jobs, Wing Puy went to Oakland to work in the shipyards.

Bennie Woon Yep arrived in the United States as a paper son at age seventeen. He was actually thirteen years old. Not speaking a word of English, he went to school during the day and worked for an American family for five years. His room consisted of a bed in the garage.

Said Bennie, "When I came from China, I was a poor boy. They gave me a job to work with an American family . . . (I) learned to cook, learned to clean house."

Bennie's talent was towards the arts, and unable to make a living as an artist he turned to sign painting. Opportunity to make a decent living arose during World War II when he was employed at Mare Island shipyard to paint signs.

One Mother Sends Six Sons Into Fig As 100 Sacramento Chinese Go to W

Edmund Yee

Edgar C. Fong

Harry Chow

Donald L. Yee   Kenneth Yee

Jacob J. Yee   David Yee

NEARLY ONE HUNDRED boys have gone from the homes of Sacramento's Chinese families to fight with the armed forces. Serving with medical detachments, army air corps ground crews, in the infantry, in fact in all branches of the service, they are stationed in all parts of the United States as well as on the world's battlefronts. Sacramento's Chinese have made their contribution to the Allied nations' war effort, a personal testimony that China is doing its part.

Three Yee families here between them have given 12 sons to fight for America. Mrs. Sam Locke Yee of 1920 20th street, a native of this city, has six sons in the war. Her late husband's father came from China and settled in Sacramento in early pioneer days. He was engaged in the butchershop business which his son carried on after his death. Mrs. Yee's sons all went into service in 1942.

PVT. RICHARD YEE, who enlisted, is stationed at Shepard field, Tex., where he is attending air corps mechanics school.

PFC. VIRGIL YEE is with the air corps administration office in Granada, Miss.

CORP. DAVID R. YEE, first of the brothers to enter the service, is an X-ray technician, stationed in Springfield, Ill., with an air corps medical detachment.

FIRST LT. DONALD L. YEE, stationed at Ft. Lewis, Wash., is also with an air corps medical detachment where he is a dentist.

SGT. EDMUND YEE is with the army air corps in England, where he is serving with a repair crew.

SGT. KENNETH YEE is stationed with a Chinese company in the army air corps and is now in Fairfield, Ohio.

Mr. and Mrs. Ging Yee, who live at 1010 U street, came here from their native China in 1918 to start a grocery business. Three of their four sons enlisted and one has seen action in four battles, while serving in the southwest Pacific and Alaska.

SEAMAN 1/C WILLIAM YEE, a tail gunner with the navy air corps, back from service in Alaska, is now stationed at Treasure Island waiting for reorders to combat duty. He enlisted in the service after graduating from high school in 1942.

PFC. DONALD YEE who also enlisted in 1942, graduated from aerial gunnery school last month in Florida. He was formerly a Richmond shipyards employe.

CORP. DAVID YEE, who was attending aerial gunnery school at Harlinger, Tex., when he entered the service in 1942, is now

with an overseas training unit at Fresno. He formerly worked at Sacramento air depot as a mechanic.

PVT. GEORGE YEE, enlisted in 1943 after graduating as licensed pharmacist from University of California. He is now with a field hospital in Florida.

MAJ. JACOB YEE, son of Mr. and Mrs. T. H. Yee of 1531 W street, is now with the 22nd field hospital in China.

Another son, PVT. HOWARD YEE, is with an aircraft artillery at Benicia.

Among many other Chinese families in Sacramento who have given their sons to the fighting forces are Mr. and Mrs. Hong Kong Chow of 1021 U street whose son, PVT. HARRY CHOW is with the 25th evacuation hospital. He entered the service in 1942 and has been in New Hebrides in the southwest Pacific since October, 1942.

Another son, COURTLAND CHOW, entered the service early in 1943 and graduated from Amarillo army air forces technical school at Idaho college, Caldwell, Idaho, for his academic phase in cadet training.

SEAMAN 2/C EDMUND FONG, husband of Mrs. Louise C. Fong, 1478 34th street, is with a naval construction battalion, decontamination and chemical warfare training unit at Camp Peary, Va.

PETTY OFFICER 2/C WILLIAM T. CHAN, husband of Mrs. Vestal L. Chan, 2314 17th street, is with the navy commissary at Williamsburg, Va.

SGT. WARREN LAI, JR., son of Mr. and Mrs. Warren Lai, Sr., 2314 17th street, is with the army air force ground crew in China.

PFC. JAMES OWYANG, brother of Mrs. Violet Lai, 2314 17th street, is with the infantry in Hawaii.

SGT. JOE JANG, son of Mr. and Mrs. G. S. Jang of Courtland, is with the air force ground crew at Fort Dix, N. J.

PFC. HOLLAND CHINN, son of Mr. and Mrs. Ned Chinn, 1320 V street, is with the air transport command in India.

PETTY OFFICER 2/C TIMOTHY S. JANG, husband of Mrs. Lilly Jang, 2317 18th street, is with Seabees in Livermore.

CORP. FOON LUM, husband of Mrs. Jennie Lum of North Sacramento, is with the second aircraft assembly squadron some-

where in the southwest.

CORP. GEORGE HIN band of Mrs. Eva Hing street, is an aviation n with army air force, Eng

S/SGT. EDWARD JOY Mr. and Mrs. L. C. Jow W street, is with a servic ron in England.

PVT. GEORGE GEORG a brother, is stationed army at Buckley field, C

CORP. MEE LEE, hus Mrs. Faustina Lee, 22 street, has been with th air force ground crew sor in the south Pacific.

A/C HERBERT LEO! band of Mrs. Edna J, I 1518 Fifth street, is w army air corps in Tempe

SGT. HERBERT S. nephew of W. S. Louje, and P streets, is with th quarters battery, anti-air tillery gunnery battalion.

FIRST LT. TUNG S. husband of Mrs. Emm 1520 N street, is with gineer intelligence sor in England.

PVT. ONG S. FONG, so and Mrs. Fong Ping, street, is attending radio at Scoffield, Ill.

SGT. EARL FONG, sor Mabel Fong, 727 N street an air corps ground cre where in England.

FIRST LT. SHUE WO band of Mrs. Frances W O street, is a dentist w medical corps at Camp

PFC. KAY WONG, son and Mrs. Jow Wong, is a in the army specialist program in San Francis

LT. ROBERT G. JAN Mrs. G. Jan, of Sacramen uated from Mather field tion school in January, 1 with a transport unit in

PFC. EDGAR FONG, of Mrs. Mabel Tom, 1832 way, is in north Africa ordnance regiment.

SGT. EDWARD J. F brother, is somewhere land with the finance ment.

CORP. DAVIS SUN, br Mrs. Minnie Moch, 1617 avenue, is with a field battalion at Fort Sill, Ok

LT. QUIN LI, former mentau, graduated from field navigation school now somewhere in the so cific.

Howard M. Yee   Donald Yee   Richard Yee   George Yee   William Yee   Virgil Yee   David R. Yee   Courtlan

(Courtesy of Chinese American Council of Sacramento)

American soldier — Hello! I'm an American soldier.

NEE EEN hah OO. waw SHR! may-GWAW BING.

China was now an ally of the United States. Therefore, the Chinese in America were comrades in arms with mainstream America. (Author's collection)

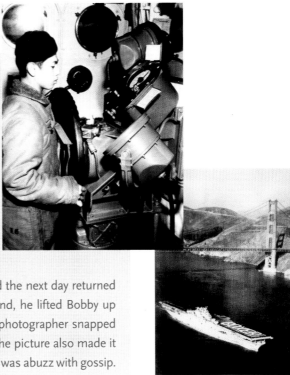

ROBERT W. H. FONG

During the Korean War, Bobby Fong (Sheu Fung Poultry) was a quartermaster on the USS Boxer. Seeing the five-foot tall Bobby steering a two hundred thousand ton aircraft carrier, stretching his neck to look out was an amusing sight. The ship's doctor, a frequent visitor on the bridge, often made fun of him. Bobby kiddingly asked, "Hey Doc! Why don't you give me some growing pills?" The doctor nodded with a smile and the next day returned with the ship's photographer. With a box in one hand, he lifted Bobby up with the other and shoved the box under him. The photographer snapped the picture and printed it in the ship's newspaper. The picture also made it to the newspapers stateside. Days later the chow line was abuzz with gossip. Letters from wives and parents with husbands or sons serving aboard the USS Boxer, were asking if they knew the five-foot tall sailor.

Five-foot tall Bobby steering the two hundred thousand ton aircraft carrier USS Boxer. (Courtesy of Robert W.H. Fong)

Old Chinatown, 1938. Looking north from Third and J Streets. The China Republic Restaurant is at 821 Third street. (Courtesy of Sacramento Archives and Museum Collection Center)

When the veterans returned home from World War II, the Chinatown they had left remained essentially unchanged.

CHAPTER ELEVEN

Leveling the Playing Field

DEMISE OF CHINATOWN

When the veterans returned home from World War II, they found the Chinatown they had left unchanged. Like its neighboring skid row, Chinatown was dying. The remaining residences were from the generation of old bachelors. In reference to the community, most agreed with Rev. Sen Wong, Pastor of the Chinese Gospel Mission at 2115 Eighth Street, when he said, ". . . I was ashamed of it."[1]

In the late 1960s, the Sacramento Redevelopment Agency designated the area bounded by Third through Fifth Streets, and by I and J Streets to be the site for a new "Oriental" center. A new era of collaboration began to take place. The Chinese now had a voice in shaping their own destiny. The "lo wah kue" (longtime overseas Chinese) Walter Fong, Fong Sik, Fong Yue Po, Marshall Jang, and Rev. Hiram Fong, longtime leaders of the community, were joined by younger members Jack C. Chew, and Howard Wong. These men joined the discussions and planning sessions with the city, designing a new Chinatown for Sacramento.

The aspirations of Sam Ong, then the President of the Chinese Benevolent Association, was to rally all the family associations together into the new center. The vision was to draw both natives and tourists back to Sacramento's west end with a cultural and commercial center of shops and restaurants.

Reflecting upon a century of discrimination and humiliation, Rev. Sen Wong said, "The new Chinatown definitely will enhance our reputation and we can lift up our heads because we have something presentable." Likewise, Rev. Hiram Fong echoed, "The Chinese in the U.S. do not often stand up and fight for a cause... The downtown project is evidence they are being forceful."[2]

Members of the community, as well as members of the public at large, praised the project. Mayor Richard H. Marriott, in his proclamation, commended the forefathers of the Chinese community for its "perseverance and incredible accomplishments" and ". . . its countless contributions . . . to the·history of Sacramento and California . . ." For the lo wah kue, this recognition was long overdue. Gum Saan, the Gold Mountain, was finally a dream fulfilled.

H. Harold Leavey, a charter member of the redevelopment agency said, ". . . the architectural design and attractiveness exceeds anything I expected."[3] Robert E. Roche, the agency's Executive Director exclaimed, " . . . it definitely looks like a real Chinatown." Architect Sooky Lee claimed it to be ". . . probably the best Chinatown in the United States."[4] The redevelopment of Chinatown was symbolic of a new era of reconciliation, a spirit of camaraderie which fostered hope, good feeling, and optimism.

South side of I Street between Second and Third Streets, 1938.

Old Chinatown, 1938. 911, 913, 915 Fourth Street. Bing Kong Tong Company was located at 911 Fourth. (Courtesy of Sacramento Archives and Museum Collection Center)

The redevelopment of Chinatown was symbolic of a new era of reconciliation; a spirit of camaraderie fostered hope, good feelings, and optimism.

On January 7, 1971, Sacramento celebrated the inauguration of the new Chinatown. The last remaining vestiges of the old Chinatown that had risen from the gold rush days was no more. Ironically, the euphoria of a new Chinatown, hailed as a new beginning, was short-lived. The transformation of the slum-like Chinatown to a commercial center was anathema to an era which emphasized the rebellious civil rights movement of the 1970s. The traditional benevolent and political organizations in their annual reports lamented the dilemma of the lack of interest from the younger generation. With great anticipation the elders had looked to the new Chinatown to bring back the reverence for the traditional values of their ancestors, only to see it denegated by the next generation as irrelevant.

The building of the Sun Yat-sen Memorial Hall was a symbol for the wah que and their decades of patriotism and passion for a new China to which this generation had no empathy. The family associations, with their new edifices designed for promotion and preservation of the culture of the ancestral land, saw instead continued drops in membership and participation. These associations, once the guiding light of the community, had diminished. The civil rights movement had ushered in a new era of optimism toward assimilation. Now moving freely within a more liberal society, American-born Chinese no longer needed to return to Chinatown to conduct business.

Courtesy of Malcolm Collier

WOMEN'S RIGHTS

Mae Chan remembers, "We were not allowed to join any (white) public or private clubs." This was in the early 1950s when the spirit of integration was not yet the norm. In order to play in "white" sponsored golf tournaments, one had to be a member of the club or association, and in order to become a member, one had to be invited.

Four women, Ling Chew, Frances Lee, Kitty Chan, and Mae Chan organized their own Chinese Women's Golf Club as an auxillary to the Chinese Men's Golf Club, which was founded for similar reasons. Dave Jan, one of the five founding members, expressed it thusly: "Let's say we were not welcomed."

Barriers were broken when these four women, one by one, were welcomed into the white clubs. The group then joined the Pacific Women's Golf Association (PWGA) which enabled them to have bona fide handicaps and to compete in the tournaments.

In 1964, Mae, an unknown, scored a major upset defeating the former city champion in a tournament. The sport section of the Sacramento Union sported the headline, "Mrs. Chan Surprises Former City Champ." For four decades, Mae competed and won major tournaments until she retired from competition in 1989.

Ling Chew, with a room full of trophies, is a testament that she was no less sensational. In 2006, at the age of ninety-three, she played in the senior tournament.

When in 1949 Eva Chan, the only Chinese to enter her name to join the bowling league at the El Camino Bowl, she was warmly welcomed.
Left to right: Nadine, Eva Chan, Kathy Paquin, Bonnie Merrill, Irene Zwohlin.
(Courtesy of Eva Chan)

Mae Chan and Ling Chew. (Author's collection)

Chinese students at William Land Park participating in International Day, 1952, an indication of the beginning of an awareness of cultural diversity.
Left to right: Dali Yee, Shirley Leong, Sally Yee, Carole Jan, Patricia Fong, Dixie Fong, Betty Chan, Jessie Lee. (Courtesy of Sacramento Archives and Museum Collection Center)

CIVIL RIGHTS MOVEMENT

Following World War II, Chinese relations improved with the community at large. World War II was clearly the turning point for socio-economic improvements for the Chinese. The push for affirmative action during the civil rights movement of the 1960s and 1970s, and the passage and enforcement of major antidiscriminatory legislation made further strides altering racial attitudes and policies.

In the past, the Chinese were able to persevere and to weather discrimination in employment and education. However, the denial of access to housing was the most unforgettable and stingingly humiliating experience. Young and old alike recalled the humiliation of looking to reside outside Chinatown, and of being rejected.

Ruby (Yuke) Fung recalled that in 1915, her father had his white kitchen supervisor purchase the house he wanted, who in turn sold it to him. Likewise, Wayne Tom had his home purchased through a white friend. Helen (Fong) Owyang was in high school when her father Fong Chuck tried to move to Land Park on Twelfth Avenue, but the agent wouldn't sell it to him. Finally he bought the house by going directly to the owner, Dr. Ernie Farrah. George Wong, who owned the Bel Air Market chain, encountered the same experience. Neighbors offered to buy him a piece of land elsewhere if he agreed not to settle in their neighborhood. When Henry Yee, the herb doctor, bought an undeveloped lot in Sierra Oaks in 1953, the neighbors tried to prevent him from building by offering to buy him a larger piece of property somewhere else. Frank Fat of restaurant fame, frustrated with his own experiences of rejection, attempted to start his own housing de-velopment. His son Wing Kai tried to buy at Sixteenth and P Streets and said, "(I) couldn't even smell the flowers there." Thomas Chinn, Bronze Star veteran of World War II recalled, "I could not buy a home in the northeast area. I could not buy a home in the southeast area . . . the picture became quite clear when one developer told me that my skin color would depreciate surrounding property values."[5] Tom was elected to be a member of the Sacramento School Board and later elected to the City Council.

Although the Chinese in America were comrades in arms with mainstream Americans during World War II, in peacetime memories were short. The prejudices of the past merely lay dormant and wartime camaraderie was left on the battlefield. Chinese could die together with whites in the same foxholes, but could not live together in the same neighborhoods. It took a war to open the doors to mainstream America; it took fair housing legislation to make it possible for the Chinese to move into the formerly restricted districts of northeast and southeast Sacramento. The passage of the United States Civil Rights Act of 1968, the UNRUH Civil Rights Act of 1989, and the California Rumford Fair Housing Act of 1963 were major factors in destroying the last bastion of discrimination.

In the period before the civil rights movement, the first generation Chinese were secure and confident with the cultural values of China, and assimilation was not a priority. The second generation, on the other hand, in order to gain acceptance into mainstream America, yielded to Anglo conformity. While World War II opened the door, the civil rights movement paved the way to equal rights and privileges and empowered minorities. Racial antipathy gradually evolved towards appreciation of cultural diversity. With these dramatic changes, the Chinese have since accessed the social, professional, business, and political community of Sacramento.

Whereas in 1858, Superintendent of Public Instruction, Andrew J. Moulder warned, "this attempt to place Africans, Chinese and Diggers into our white schools . . . must result in the ruin of our schools." Today, the Chinese are among the principals and teachers in the public schools. Furthermore, Tom Chinn was elected to the School Board of Sacramento in 1972, followed by Joanne Yee in 1988.

Since the momentous days of James Marshall's discovery of gold in Coloma, the history of medicine in Sacramento had not recorded a single physician of Chinese descent until Dr. Lung Fung arrived in Sacramento in 1934. Dr. Fung, a native of Sebastopol, California, was a track star at Analy High School and enjoyed the reputation of being the "fastest human in Sonoma County." He graduated from the Stanford University School of Medicine, passed his state exams, and was ready to start his practice in San Francisco's Chinatown when a pharmacist friend, Wingo Wye from San Francisco, cautioned him that "there's tens of Chinese physicians here, better go to Sacramento." His advice proved not to be the answer either. Dr. Fung opened his office on 1116½ Seventh Street and wife Ruby remembered, "He sat there cleaning his fingernails," and surmised that when the Chinese wanted western medicine they preferred a Caucasian doctor, not a stranger in town.

Bills had to be paid, so for a short term, Dr. Fung entered a contract as surgeon with the Civilian Conservation Corps at Camp

Kerby, Oregon. In November of 1935, he resumed his practice at his office in Sacramento. With the advent of World War II, Dr. Fung took his physical examination for military service, but was disqualified and unaccepted because he was afflicted with asthma and hay fever. His inclination to serve his country was fulfilled when he was appointed medical examiner for the local draft board.

While Dr. Fung was contemplating his move to Sacramento, his friend Wingo Wye introduced him to Dan Yuke, a Sacramento dentist. His luck took a turn for the better when he met Ruby, Dan's sister, who was cooking spaghetti for the family. Was it Ruby's thrill at meeting a Stanford graduate, or was it Ruby's spaghetti that thrilled the doctor? In any case, they began dating and continued until after Ruby graduated from the University of California, Berkeley. In 1938, Fung said to Ruby, "Let's get married." Their honeymoon was going to the Big Game, the annual football game between rival Stanford and UC Berkeley teams.

By 1970, Dr. Fung had moved his office into the Ping Yuen housing center in new Chinatown where he remained until retirement on December 31, 1975, having served the community for forty years.

The second Chinese physician to practice in Sacramento was Dr. George Yee from San Francisco in 1948. Not all members at Mercy General or Sutter Hospital were receptive to having a Chinese doctor on staff. Dr. Yee was shockingly awakened to the reality of prejudice when he was advised by a Caucasian physician, "Why don't you go back to your own people." That same physician must have really been upset when by the 1950s, seven more physicians of Chinese descent served

DR. EDNA MAE FONG

When she attended to her patient in his room, the cleaning woman reported to the front desk, "Get that Chinese woman out of there; this is not visiting hour!"

the Sacramento community. They were doctors Leslie Lee, Carl Fong, Evan Fong, Gaing Chan, Franklin Chinn, William Fong and the first Chinese woman doctor, Edna Mae Fong.[6]

If George Yee found acceptance difficult, it took tremendous courage for a woman doctor like Dr. Edna Mae Fong to survive. When she started her pediatric practice in the late 1940s, she did not receive referrals from other doctors. She took on work in the mornings, visiting the well baby clinic sixty miles away, then drove back to the office for the afternoons, and worked in the emergency room at the city jail in the evenings.

Night guards at Sutter and Mercy General, unconvinced she was a doctor, harassed her and refused to let her in. Once, when she attended to a patient in his room, the cleaning woman reported to the front desk, "Get that 'Chinese' woman out of there; this is not visiting hour!" The ultimate insult was while she was scrubbing up, a male Caucasian doctor attempted to pull down her pants. Dr. Fong, with a sigh of resignation reflected, "I worked hard for my money!"

Currently there are physicians of Chinese descent in nearly every discipline and subspecialty and administrative capacity. Of special note are Dr. William Fong, who became Chief of Staff at Mercy General Hospital, Trustee of the Sutter Hospital, and the California Medical Association; and Dr. Gaing Chan, who also served as Chief of Staff at Mercy General Hospital.[7]

Along with the Chinese expansion into different professions, those with an entrepreneurial spirit entered into a broad range of businesses. In his seventy-eight years in America, Frank Fat's experiences typify those of the first generation. Coming to America in 1919 at age sixteen as a paper son and assuming the name of Wong Bing Yuen, he took jobs washing dishes at the Sutter Club, worked for Dong Haw at the Hong King Lum Restaurant, picked fruit in the delta, and worked in a laundry.

Finally in 1939, Frank with Dong Haw and a friend bought a former Italian restaurant and speakeasy bar at 806 L Street. The Frank Fat culinary legend was born. Because of the proximity to the State Capitol, Frank Fat's restaurant became a favorite location where important legislative business was brokered over lunch and dinner. Through his restaurant, Frank got to know every governor who occupied the State Capitol.

The restaurant had a favored booth where legislators wanted to be seated in order to watch who came in. It was nicknamed the "Judge Garibaldi Booth" after the big time lobbyist. It was also known as the "power booth." Frank's son, Wing Kai chuckled with a grin from ear to ear when he told the story of how he told Governor Jerry Brown Jr., where he could or could not sit in his restaurant. One day Governor Brown walked in and sat himself in the power booth. Wing Kai said, "Governor Brown, you can't sit here, it's taken," proving the old adage "He who laughs last laughs best." Today Frank Fat's legacy is carried on by five generations of family members.

Frank Fat, restaurateur, passed away on April 5, 1997, at the age of ninety-three. Condolences and messages of tribute were sent to the family from the very same offices of lawmakers, which over a century ago had passed acrimonious anti-Chinese ordinances and legislation designed to prevent Chinese people like Frank from immigrating. The City Council of Sacramento sent a resolution in memory of Frank Fat. The Los Angeles County Board of Supervisors adjourned its meeting of May 20, 1997 in tribute and reverence of the memory of Frank Fat. United States Supreme Court Justice Anthony M. Kennedy, California Supreme Court Associate Justice Joyce L. Kennard, and then President of the United States Bill Clinton likewise sent their condolences.

Veterans returning home following V-E Day shared in an era of good feeling and good will. After two years in the European Theatre of War, Joe Wayne Fong returned home thankful he was alive. Prior to entering into the service, he had worked in his father's laundry. Joe emphatically boasted, "I used to iron shirts, twelve an hour! Not with an electric iron, with an iron heated over a stove! You have to know the heat. I never burned a shirt!"

Skillful as he was, ironing shirts for the rest of his life like his father was not for him. In a new climate of optimism, there were options. Joe decided he would go into the service station business. He and brothers Bob and Jack purchased the station on Eleventh and S Streets and named it Wayne's Auto Service, pioneering the Chinese owned gas station enterprise in town. In 1958, Joe sold his share of the business to Bob and opened the Flying A on Sixth and P Streets, and finally opened a parking garage at Seventh and R Streets.

In 1958, Paul Fong and wife Mae operated in their home at Seventh and P Streets a small printing business with only two duplicators. Paul would work all day while Mae would come in the afternoon after finishing her morning teaching job at the Westfield Elementary School in West Sacramento. Their husband and wife team printing business has since expanded into a multi-million dollar operation at the 3009 Sixty-fifth Street facility, where high tech equipment produces high caliber products.

Paul Fong originally worked for Pacific Lithographers as an artist while in high school. With men going off to war in 1941, Paul was put to work in the production end of the business. With his draft number coming up, he enlisted and was assigned to the United States Army Engineer Corps, in the map making mobile unit, producing maps for troops who had secured and occupied enemy territory during the Normandy/Omaha Beach invasion. After World War II, Paul returned and worked for Sacramento Lithographers, ending up as manager and after twelve years opted to venture on his own. For Paul's wife Mae, it was an excellent opportunity to put her degree in economics to work, along with her business acumen. After she spent years earning a degree in economics, it was still difficult to find a job so she ended up teaching. Mae said, "My desire was to go into business.

In the era of good feelings and goodwill following World War II, the Chinese were no longer limited to being domestic servants, cooks, and laundrymen. Joe Wing Fong returned home not to work in his father's laundry, but entered into the service station business with his brothers Bob and Jack.

Fong's laundry on Sutter Street in Folsom, California. (Courtesy of Joe Wayne Fong)

Wayne's Auto Service at Eleventh and S Streets in Sacramento. Joe and Bob started a service station and auto repair business. (Courtesy of Joe Wayne Fong)

I couldn't get a job." "At that time it was less critical (finding a teaching job); they were hiring Chinese girls."

Today Fong & Fong Printers & Lithographers is still family owned and operated with son Curtis as Executive Vice President, and daughters Marsha, Vice President of Operations, and Karen, Vice President of Finance. They currently run the business, providing employment to 130 employees.

Mae has been the recipient of the Sacramento Metropolitan Chamber of Commerce's Distinguished Businesswoman's Award in 1981. Participating in over fifty years of Masonic activities, Paul served as the illustrious potentate of Sacramento's Ben Ali Temple in 1989.

Paul Fong. (Courtesy of Mae Fong)

The Fong's entrepreneurial spirit is matched only by their philanthropic spirit. Mae has sat on the Board of Directors for Junior Achievement, the Sacramento Area Trade and Commerce Organization, the Sacramento Zoological Society, the American Red Cross, and the United Way.

In city and county government, further barriers were broken. Sun G. Wong was elected and served on the City Council from 1966–1971, followed by Tom Chinn from 1982–1992, and Jimmie Yee in 1992. Subsequently, Jimmie Yee became the first Chinese Mayor of Sacramento. The first time Jimmie ran for City Council, he walked the Land Park district, an exclusive white area, accompanied by a Caucasian to ring the front door bell of residences as an insurance they would open their doors. Fifteen years later, Jimmie was elected to County Supervisor without resorting to similar tactics. In 1986, Roger Fong ran for the Office of County Assessor and became not only the first Chinese but the only minority ever elected to a countywide office. While campaigning and riding in a parade in Rio Linda, he was confronted with, "Hey, Chinaman, what are you doing here?" On another occasion while handing out flyers, a person candidly remarked, "I don't vote for Orientals." Amongst members of the legislative system are Municipal Court Judge Cheryl Chun Meegan (appointed in 1994) and Municipal Court Commissioner Patricia Wong.

Dr. Herbert Yee, following the tradition of his father, herb doctor Henry Yee, is a leading candidate for serving on commissions and boards beyond his own ethnic community. To name a few of his honors, Governor Edmund G. Brown appointed him to the State Dental Board; he was appointed to the University of the Pacific Regents; and in 1985, he was the President representing the United States membership in the International College of Dentistry.

While the Chinese in Sacramento had

The company's large manufacturing facility on a five-acre site at 65th Street and Broadway, designed by architect Sooky Lee.

FONG KING CHUNG

Paul's father, Fong King Chung, came to the United States as a "paper son." He remembers his father telling him the age of the person he was supposed to impersonate was older than he was, and therefore he let his hair grow to look older. This helped his entry and he immediately went to Sacramento where his "paper father" lived.

It was a good move and while Fong was attending the Baptist Church to learn English, Mrs. Glide, a prominent Yolo County landowner, came to find a person willing to learn to cook for the Glide family household. The Glides were known for throwing lavish parties at their 4100 Folsom Boulevard estate to entertain military personnel from the air base. When Fong was ready to retire, the next generation of Glides urged him to stay on. Fong ended up as chef for three generations of the Glide family. During this time, he and his wife, Mee Lee, raised six children: Paul, Hugh, Peggy, Ben, June, and Yung.

begun to move into politics and were enjoying the benefits of equal opportunity fomented by the civil rights movement, that movement also inspired a group of young college students at Sacramento State College, Sacramento City College, and the University of California, Davis to aspire to a broader consciousness of activism. In concert with other Asian Americans, African Americans, Hispanics, and Native Americans, this new consciousness held forth regarding social concerns, political controversies of the Vietnam War, United States/China relations, and the Cold War.

Said Ray Lee, "These were tumultuous times!" as he recognized the profound changes that were taking place across the nation. The more conservative and passive elements of the community disapproved, and viewed the activities as a result of communist infiltration. Ray's father called him a communist. Harold Fong's father was upset and admonished him for wasting his time instead of pursuing his education. On the other hand, Marion Ono, a social worker said, "I was electrified by the Free Speech movement!" Marion grew up in the generation which endured the wrath of discrimination in silence. While working with a psychiatric team, she inquired at the Chinese Housing Project whether there was a need for a Chinese speaking person. Queen Wallace, known as the "Dragon Lady," took her to an organizational meeting where she met Ray and Harold. Said Marion, "They roped me in . . . trained me to speak (up) provided an outlet (for my anger)."

Organized as the Peace One Collective, eight people who believed in the motto, "Serve the People," organized and ran much needed free mental and children health

Left to right: Marion Ono, Ray Lee, Harold Fong

clinics. They were aided by cannery workers, manpower programs for job placement, legal services supported by students from the University of the Pacific Law School, and tutorial programs tutored by students attending the local colleges.

UC Davis runs the Health Center, which had its beginnings with the Peace One Collective. One member of the collective, Paul Hom, was honored for his role in founding the Health Center. The credit in the founding of their organization and the "know how" to tap and utilize Federal resources to serve the people belongs to those eight people and their vision.

Harold Fong formed the Third World Alliance at Sacramento State, which demanded establishment of Ethnic Studies programs at Sacramento City College and at UC Davis.

Prohibition of Chinese testimony against a white person and the denial of rights to citizenship, equal employment, and equal housing may seem to be distant history. However, with neo-Nazi organizations, such as the National Alliance, declaring America must be white, racism in the twenty-first century has yet to be fully resolved. As a case in point, when Jimmie Yee was Mayor of Sacramento, his house was firebombed. For weeks Mayor Yee performed his duties wearing a bullet-proof vest and accompanied by special bodyguards. His wife Mary did likewise. Fearful of further attacks on minority officials, Assessor Roger Fong requested and was given a concealed gun permit.

On May 17, 1984, the Human Rights/Fair Housing Commission of the City and County of Sacramento conducted a hearing on the bigotry and violence against Pacific Americans. The Sacramento County Sheriff's Department provided these statistics: In 1983, of the eighty reported, thirty-five were racially motivated. Between January to April 1984, Indo-Chinese filed thirty-four reports of crime, of which eleven were racially motivated.

A national survey conducted in 2001 by Yankelovich Partners, in collaboration with the Anti-Defamation League and the Marttila Communications Group, revealed that one out of four Americans would feel uncomfortable voting for an Asian American for President of the United States. The same percentage would disapprove of a family member marrying someone of Asian descent. Seventeen percent said they would be upset if a substantial number of Asians moved into their neighborhood.[8]

Since 1975, the United States has accepted over 657,000 Indo-Chinese immigrants of which over 300,000 have chosen to live in California. About 15,000 live in the City and County of Sacramento. They are Vietnamese, Chinese, Mung from Vietnam, Khmer from Cambodia, Hmong and Mien from Laos.

DEMOGRAPHY AND DIVERSITY

The civil rights movement of the 1960s and 1970s raised the consciousness of Chinese America and inspired discussion on racism and discrimination versus acculturation and assimilation. Frequently discussed is what makes a person growing up in Sacramento different from one growing up in San Francisco? The personalities in Chinese America are complex, not homogeneous. The experiences growing up Chinese in America varies from generation to generation and are determined by population density within a given time and place.

One of the perceived differences is in the behavioral patterns influenced by acculturation and assimilation. The process and pace of assimilation is governed by the numerical ratio of the Chinese minority dwelling among the white majority, the number of generations settled in America, and the response of the white majority to the presence of the Chinese, all coincident with changing politics over time.

The first generation Chinese in the nineteenth and early twentieth century faced blatant racism when laws and legislation were passed with the purpose to deny assimilation. For many second generation Chinese, assimilation often meant adopting Anglo American values while rejecting their own cultural roots. By the third generation and beyond, a more tolerant environment encouraged assimilation without the demands to reject one's Chinese culture.

From the 1870s up to the 1906 earthquake, San Francisco was obsessed with the annihilation of Chinatown and its population. Chinatown was a refuge, a place protected against discrimination. The duration of hostile attitudes and actions which contained and isolated the Chinese population from participating in the mainstream continued, while over the same period, because of the small number of Chinese in Sacramento, hostilities began to subside. Hostility was also ameliorated with the immigration of a large number of Japanese. In the early 1900s, large numbers of Japanese began to farm and buy agricultural land in the Sacramento valley. Their presence once again alarmed the general public of a "Yellow Peril." Governor William D. Stephens wrote, "The Japanese in our midst have indicated a strong trend to land ownership . . . and . . . have gradually developed to a control of many of our important agricultural resources . . ."9

Anti-Japanese hostilities not only directed attention away from the Chinese, the Chinese were now considered to be more favorable than the Japanese. Historian Bancroft wrote, "for common labor, factory work, and fruit farming, industries necessary to our civilization . . . the Chinaman has no equal. He is faithful, efficient, and honest, he is clearly thrifty, and decent." And he wrote, "The Japanese . . . is captious, clamorous of his rights and would like to become the equal or superior of the white race."10

The establishment of Chinese-owned supermarkets in the 1930s was not only an economic advancement, but as employers, they were goodwill ambassadors narrowing the social distance between whites and Chinese. Unlike the typical Chinese markets located within the confines of the Chinese quarters of Sacramento, Chinese supermarkets were established beyond their ethnic boundaries, and catered to mainstream citizens of Sacramento. The presence of second generation managers and employees was a breakthrough in dispelling the foreign non-assimilable imagery of the previous generation. The nondiscriminatory employment practices of the Chinese management further promoted goodwill, especially in the years of the Depression.

Improved immigration policies enacted in the 1950s and 1960s brought continuous renewal of the numbers of first generation Chinese. Unlike the earlier immigrants, these newcomers could choose where they wished to settle. The less affluent immigrants, by economic necessity, gravitated towards an environment with familiar customs. The Chinatowns of New York, Los Angeles, and San Francisco provided a place where Chinese was still spoken as the primary language. Perpetual arrival of first generations give assurance that Chinese culture is maintained and nurtured.

Although the foreign-born and native-born alike live throughout the city in San Francisco, many continue to have contact with the Chinese community, returning to shop, to work, to serve in community organizations, and to participate in community events. The Chinese influence is not only in Chinatown but is present throughout the city. The behavioral patterns of the Chinese in San Francisco spans from the alien population adhering to their cultural traditions, to those native-born who embrace their cultural identity, and to those who have completely adopted values of Anglo America.

Sacramento, on the other hand, no longer is the magnet it was in the days of the gold rush. The Chinese quarters that rose from the gold rush vanished with the city's redevelopment. For the small number of recent newcomers who choose to settle in Sacramento, there is no identifiable ethnic center to gravitate to. The social distance between the foreign-born and their offspring with the longtime residents is too far apart for mutual socialization. Therefore, the new immigrants chose to establish their own ethnic enclave. Evidence of this separation from American-born Chinese is the Sacramento Chinese Indo-China Friendship Association, with a Chinese temple and language school on 6117 Elder Creek Road.

Without strong cultural reminders, the cultural roots of the longtime residents have diminished. Living comfortably throughout the city, and working daily with mainstream Sacramentans have shaped their behavioral characteristics. Their lifestyle is comfortably that of mainstream America and of Sacramento.

*New Vietnamese Chinese
immigrants chose to establish
their own ethnic enclave
with their own market,
Chinese school and temple on
6117 Elder Creek Road.*

Market.

Chinese school.

*Today Sacramento's population
is by no means monolithic.*

Temple.

To maintain Chinese cultural traditions, the Chinese Community Church celebrates the "Fifth Day of the Fifth Month" (Dragon Boat Festival) by making "joong" (rice wrapped with bamboo leaves).

Chinese American Council of Sacramento honors Jimmie Yee. Left to right: Chee Fat, Jimmie and Mary Yee, Wing Kai Fat. (Courtesy of Karun Yee)

Chinese American Council of Sacramento and the Sacramento Chinese Community Service Center participating in Pacific Rim Street Festival. From left to right: Karun Yee, Doug Yee, Dolly Louie, Alfred Yee, Shu Yeh. (Courtesy of Karun Yee)

The Mandarins Drum and Bugle Corps began in 1963 as an all-Chinese drum corps named "Yee Wah" founded by Roy Wong, Frank Lim, Thomas Fong and Yuk Fong. Symbolic of the progress of time, the nationally-renowned organization is noticeably integrated with only a handful of Chinese.

(Courtesy of Scott Jow)

EPILOGUE

Until the repeal of the Exclusion Act on December 17, 1943, the Chinese in America were predominantly from Guangdong province centered about the Pearl River delta. The nation's involvement in Asia brought about more immigration, fostering a diverse population from all parts of Asia. Besides the Cantonese organizations of yesteryear, the founding of the Sacramento Area Formosan Association, the Overseas Chinese of America, and the Sacramento Chinese Indo-China Friendship Association, bears evidence that Sacramento's Chinese population community is by no means monolithic.

The coming of new immigrants coincided with the nation's civil rights movement. In a little over six decades since the repeal of the Exclusion Act, tremendous strides had been made in the Chinese community. Today, for the vast majority of the present generation of Chinese who has never seen the Chinatown of "old" nor experienced living during the exclusion era, it is difficult to imagine not being allowed to sit in the main floor of a theatre, not being able to enter a swimming pool with your Anglo-American friends (if you had any), and of being rejected when looking for a place to rent or to buy, and being rejected for employment based on the color of your skin.

Today there are over ninety-five organizations representing not only the Chinese in Sacramento, but all Asians, including Pacific Islanders, with the mission to provide, promote, and support programs for health, education, employment, leadership, and citizenship. The publication of the nonprofit quarterly newspaper *Current* supported calls of attention to issues of racism and hate crimes yet to be resolved in our twenty-first century. Recently Linda Ng of the Overseas Chinese of America and Dr. Sonney Chong and Alice Wong of the Council of Asian Pacific Islanders Together for Advocacy and Leadership, singled out preventing and illuminating hate crimes to be their organization's top priority.

On a more positive note, all organizations are in agreement with the Sacramento Chinese Community Service Center in its philosophy "while adopting a new culture honor the old." While cultural maintenance is ideologically worthwhile, the reality is that it will inevitably diminish within two or more generations under pressures of assimilation and as Asians become partners in the social, economic, and political processes of Sacramento. Second generation George Quan, Jr. observed with optimism, "We are entering a new era. My grandchildren's surnames are Soberquist and Joyce." For the Chinese the cultural pendulum has swung from Anglo dominance to acknowledging ethnic diversity in defining who is American. Second generation Margaret (Fong) Lum concluded, "Although ethnicity is now on the upswing, we consider ourselves Americans though Chinese." Similarly, second generation Russell Fong noted, "It is now fashionable to be a minority." The names Yee, Fong, and Nguyen are as American as McClatchy, Dukmejian, and Schwarzenegger.

Today, Cantonese footprints are found throughout the California landscape: in the high Sierra, in the Sacramento and San Joaquin Delta, and in the generations of families living in Sacramento.

NOTES

CHAPTER ONE America and the Far East

1. Josiah Quincy, *The Journals of Major Samuel Shaw* (Boston: Wm. Crosby And H.P. Nichols, 111 Washington Street, 1847), 163.

2. Ibid., 183.

3. Ibid., 231.

4. Tyler Dennett, *Americans In Eastern Asia* (New York: The Macmillion Company, 1922), 555.

CHAPTER TWO Western Imperialism and Internal Disorder

1. Frederic Wakeman, Jr., *The Fall of Imperial China* (The Free Press, A Division of Macmillan Publishing Co.,Inc., New York and Collier Macmillion Publishers, London, 1975), 155.

CHAPTER THREE Leaving Home

1. Sandford Fleming, *God's Gold* (Philadelphia: The Judson Press, 1949), 177.

2. Watt Steward, *Chinese Bondage in Peru, A History of the Chinese Coolie In Peru*, 1840 (Durham, North Carolina: Duke University Press, 1951), 125.

3. *Daily Alta California*, July 19, 25, 1854.

CHAPTER FOUR Yee Fow, The Second City

1. Jerry Mac Mullen, *Paddle-Wheel Days in California* (Stanford University Press, Stanford California, 1970), 6.

2. Rev. William Taylor, *California Life Illustrated* (London: Jackson, Walford, and Hadder, 1867), 104.

3. J. W. Woolridge, *History of the Sacramento Valley California* (Chicago: The Pioneer Historical Publishing Co. Vol. 1; 1931), 131.

4. *Alta California*, May 18, 1851, p. 1:3.

5. Rev. William Speer, *An Humble Plea* (San Francisco, *The Oriental*, 1856), 18.

6. Mary Praetzellis and Adrian Praetzellis, *Historical Archeology of an Overseas Chinese Community in Sacramento, California* (Anthropological Studies Center, Sonoma State University Academic Foundation Inc., Rohnert Park, CA Feb. 1997), 64.

7. Correspondence from Anthropological Studies Center.

8. California Historical Society, San Francisco, CA., MS 39 (Vault) Vol. 1.

9. J. A. Benton, *California Pilgrim* (Sacramento, Cal: Solomon Center Alter Publisher: Marvin & Hitchcock, San Francisco, 1853), 164.

10. The author has copies of the documents from the recorder's office in Storey County, Nevada, to verify existence of the incident here-in told by Albert Dressler.

11. Albert Dressler, "The Medical Certificate of Dr. Wah Hing," *The Westerner* (July 1930), 6.

12. Benton, *California Pilgrim*, 140.

13. *Alta California*, Apr. 13, 1857, 2:3.

14. *Alta California*, Aug. 3, 1859.

15. Taylor, *California Life*, 340.

16. In the 1878 Well Fargo Chinese Business Directory, I Street was designated as "Tong Yun Gai" in Chinese characters. The name was continuously used by local residences up to the time of the City's re-development in the 1960's.

17. *American Memory, 19th Century in Print*. View 148 Letter from Chin Toy of Sacramento. *The American Missionary*, Vol. 39, May 5, 1885.

18. Condit, *The Chinatown As We See Him* (Fleming H. Revell Company, Chicago, New York, Toronto 1990), 181–185.

19. Wells Fargo 1878 Chinese Business Directory used the term "Sah-gah-meen-do" (Sacramento) in Chinese characters and in the 1882 directory changed the use to Yee Fow (second city).

CHAPTER FIVE Moving Earth and Mountain

1. "Chinese Immigration, Its Social, Moral, and Political Effect" Report to the State of California, Sacramento: State Printing Office, 1878.

2. Theodore H. Hittell, *History of California* (San Francisco: W. J. Stone & Company, Vol. 4, 1897), 104

3. George Chu, "Chinatown in the Delta: The Chinese in the Sacramento-San Joaquin Delta, 1870–1960," *The California Historical Society Quarterly* (March 1970), 23.

4. Report of Committees of the Senate of the United States for the second Session of the 44th Congress. Washington: Government Printing Office, 1877.

5. C. Crocker, C.P.R.R. Pay Roll No. 26, Jan. 1864. On file at California, State Railroad Museum Library, Sacramento, California.

6. George Kraus, *High Road to Promontory* (Palo Alto, California: American West Publishing Company, 1969), 248.

7. Hittel, *History of California*, 480.

CHAPTER SIX The Great Divine

1. H. Brett Melendy and Benjamin F. Gilbert, *The Governors of California* (Georgetown, California, The Talisman Press, 1965), 133.

2. Melendy, *The Governors*, 149.

3. Lucile Eaves, *A History of California Labor Legislation* (Berkeley, The University Press, 1910), 140.

4. Eaves, *California Labor*, 141.

5. *Sacramento Union*, March 2, 1882, 3:3.

6. Ibid., Jan. 18, 1886, 2:3.

CHAPTER SEVEN Emigration and Immigration Restriction

1. *Washington Times*, Jan. 1, 1902.

2. J. B. Sawyer, Procedure in Section 6" And Other Chinese Immigration Matters (Washington: Government Printing Office, 1924).

3. Ibid., 21–24

4. Rule 33 of the *Laws, Treating and Regulations Relating To The Exclusion Of The Chinese* (Washington Printing Office 1903), 41.

5. Tally from the 1913 International Chinese Business Directory of the World excluding herb shops and restaurants.

6. *Congressional Record*, Mar. 19-Apr. 9, 1910, 4083.

7. Elsie O. Yun & Stephen Yun, editors, 1993 Delta Reunion, (Sept. 25, 1999) MS (unpublished).

CHAPTER EIGHT From Mom & Pop to Super-Marts

1. *Chinese Digest*, May 29, 1936, 3:2.

2. Alfred Yee, *Shopping At Giant Foods* (University of Washington Press, 2003), 104.

CHAPTER NINE Wah Que and Jook Sing

1. *San Francisco Chronicle*, Feb. 14, 1906, 2.2.

2. *Evening Bulletin*, May 2, 1900, 6:1.

3. Chen Kwong Min, *The Chinese In The Americas* (Overseas Chinese Culture Publication Co., New York, N.Y. 1950), 113.

4. Ibid., 115.

5. "Articles of Incorporation of the Confucius Church of Sacramento" Chinese Benevolent Association of Sacramento Commemorative Chinese Publication, 1997, 4–8.

6. *San Francisco Chronicle*, Jan. 21, 1905, 5.

7. Joel Franks, "Chinese Americans and American Sport 1884–1940" in *Chinese America: History and Perspectives* (San Francisco: Chinese Historical Society of America, 1996), 135.

8. Loren A. McIntyre, "Eight Thousand Mile Field Trip," *California Monthly* (Nov. 1941), 21.

9. Statistic of Chinese Churches, Mission, Schools and Institutions of North America, 1892.

10. From the article on the History of the Baptist Church written in Chinese by Rev. Lee Shaw Yan, who served in 1930, n.d.

11. Estella Sutton Aitchison, "A Winter Tour In the Land of Sunshine: The Baptist Home Mission Monthly (1921), 15.

12. John W. Hurst. "Hiram Fong's Family Numbers Almost 3,000," *Sacramento Bee*, 1969.

13. Article on the "History of the Chinese Community Church: written in Chinese by Rev. Kwok Wei Sing, 50, 51 n.d.

14. *San Francisco Chronicle*, Aug. 15, 1931, 5:6.

15. From the article "On The History of the Chinese Community Church," Chicago, Ill. (The World Service Methodist Episcopal Church, 1931) pamphlet 16.

16. Chen Kwong Min, *The Chinese in the Americas* (New York, N.Y. 1950), 113, 115.

17. Ibid., 133. The names of the twenty in attendance were listed in Chinese.

CHAPTER ELEVEN Leveling the Playing Field

1. *Sacramento Bee*, Jan. 17, 1971, 47:2.

2. Ibid., 47:1.

3. Ibid., 8:4.

4. Ibid., 8:4.

5. Ibid., 32:2.

6. Franklin Yee, M.D., "The History of Chinese Medicine in Sacramento" (Feb. 25, 1991) MS (unpublished).

7. Ibid.

8. *San Francisco Chronicle*, April 27, 2001

9. *California And The Oriental, Japanese, Chinese, and Hindus*. Report of the State of California to Gov. Wm. O. Stephens. (California State Printing Office, Sacramento, Jan. 1, 1922), 8.

10. Hubert Howe Bancroft, *Retrospection Political and Personal* (New York, Bancroft Co. 1915), 357.

EPILOGUE

1. Conversation with George Quan, Jr., San Francisco, Sept. 17, 2006.

2. Margaret Lum, "Life As A Chinese American," Unpublished autobiography, Dixon, California, n.d.

3. Russell S. Fong, Chinese Community Church, RCA Unpublished Notes. Sacramento. Jan. 21, 1989.

BIBLIOGRAPHY

50th Anniversary 1910–1960. San Francisco: Young China Morning Paper, 1960.

Aldus, Don. *Coolie Traffic and Kidnapping*. London: McCorquodale & Co., "The Armoury," 1876.

Barber & Baker. *Sacramento Illustrated*. Sacramento: Reprint of original edition issued 1855, Sacramento Book Collectors Club, 1950.

Bau, Mingchien Joshua. *The Open Door Doctrine in Relation to China*. New York: Macmillan, 1923.

Borthwick, J. D. *Three Years in California*. Oakland: Biobooks, 1948.

Chan, Sucheng. *This Bitter-Sweet Soil: The Chinese in California Agriculture, 1860–1910*. Berkeley: University of California Press, 1986.

Chen, Ta. United States Department of Labor, Bureau of Labor Statistics: Chinese Migrations, with Special Reference to Labor Conditions. Taipei, Taiwan: Ch'eng Wen Publishing, 1967.

Chiu, Ping. *Chinese Labor in California, An Economic Study*. Madison: University of Wisconsin, 1967.

Choy, Philip P., Lorraine Dong, and Marlon K. Hom. *The Coming Man: 19th Century American Perceptions of the Chinese*. Hong Kong: Joint Publishing (H.K.) Co., 1994.

Condit, Ira M. *The Chinaman as We See Him and Fifty Years of Work for Him*. Chicago: Fleming H. Revell, 1900.

Coolidge, Mary Roberts. *Chinese Immigration*. New York: Henry Holt, 1909.

Cross, Ira B. *A History of the Labor Movement in California*. Berkeley: University of California Press, 1915.

Crossman, Carl L. *The China Trade: Export Paintings, Furniture, Silver and Other Objects*. Princeton: Pyne Press, 1972.

Davis, Winfield J., *History of Political Conventions*. Sacramento: Publication of the California State Library, No. 1, 1893.

Deane, Hugh. *Good Deeds & Gunboats, Two Centuries of American-Chinese Encounters*. San Francisco: China Books & Periodicals, 1990.

Denker, Ellen Paul. *After the Chinese Taste: China's Influence in America, 1730–1930*. Salem, MA: Peabody Museum, 1985.

Dennett, Tyler. *Americans in Eastern Asia*. New York: Macmillan, 1922.

Dulles, Foster Rhea. *The Old China Trade, American Maritime History*. New York: Library Editions, 1970.

Eaves, Lucile. *A History of California Labor Legislation with an Introductory Sketch of the San Francisco Labor Movement*. Berkeley: The University Press, 1966.

Elsbree, Oliver Wendell. *The Rise of the Missionary Spirit in America, 1790–1815*. Philadelphia: Porcupine Press, 1980.

Fairbank, John King. *Trade and Diplomacy on the China Coast, The Opening of the Treaty Ports, 1842–1854*. Stanford University Press, 1969.

Farkas, Lani Ah Tye. *Bury My Bones In America: The Saga of a Chinese Family in California 1852–1996: From San Francisco to the Sierra Gold Mines*. Nevada City, CA: Carl Mautz, 1998.

Fisher, Lloyd H. *The Harvest Labor Market in California*. Cambridge: Harvard University Press, 1953.

Fleming, Sanford. *God's Gold: The Story of Baptist Beginnings in California 1849–1860*. Philadelphia: Judson Press, 1949.

Ford, Eddy Lucius. *The History of the Educational Work of the Methodist Episcopal Church in China: A Study of Its Development and Present Trends*. Foochow, China: Christian Herald Mission, 1938.

Foster, John W. *American Diplomacy in the Orient*. Cambridge: Houghton Mifflin, 1903.

Fritz, Christian. *Federal Justice in California The Court of Odgen Hoffman, 1851–1891*. Lincoln: University of Nebraska, 1991.

Gammell, William. *The Story of American Baptist Missions*. Boston: Gould, Kendall and Lincoln, 1849.

Gernet, Jacques. *A History of Chinese Civilization,* Vol. I and II. London: Folio Society, 2002.

Goldstein, Jonathan. *Philadelphia and the China Trade, 1682–1846*. University Park: Pennsylvania State University, 1978.

Griswold, Wesley S. *A Work of Giants: Building the First Transcontinental Railroad*. New York: McGraw-Hill, 1962.

Gulick, Edward V. *Peter Parker and the Opening of China*. Cambridge: Harvard University Press, 1973.

Gulick, Sidney L. *American Democracy and Asiatic Citizenship*. New York: Charles Scribner's Sons, 1918.

Hibbert, Christopher. *The Dragon Wakes China and the West, 1793–1911*. New York: Harper & Row, 1970.

Howard, David Sanctuary. *New York and the China Trade*. The New-York Historical Society, 1984.

Howard, Robert West. *The Great Iron Trail: The Story of the First Transcontinental Railroad*. New York: Bonanza Books, 1962.

Hu, Sheng. *Imperialism and Chinese Politics*. Peking, China: Foreign Languages Press, 1955.

Hunter, W. C. *The 'Fan Kwae' at Canton Before Treaty Days, 1825–1844*. Taipei, Taiwan: Ch'eng-wen Publishing, reprint 1965.

Jenkins, John E. *The Coolie: His Rights and Wrongs*. New York: George Routledge & Sons, 1871.

Konvitz, Milton R. *The Alien and the Asiatic in American Law*. Ithaca, NY: Cornell University, 1946.

Kraus, George. *High Road to Promontory*. Palo Alto, CA: American West, 1969.

Krausse, Alexis. *China in Decay: The Story of a Disappearing Empire*. London: Chapman & Hall, 1990.

Kung, Chuan Hsiao. *Rural China, Imperial Control in the Nineteenth Century*. Seattle: University of Washington Press, 1960.

Lai, Him Mark, Genny Lim, and Judy Yung. *Island: Poetry and History of Chinese Immigrants on Angel Island, 1910–1940*. Seattle: University of Washington Press, 1980.

Lambert, Frank. *Inventing the "Great Awakening."* Princeton, NJ: Princeton University Press, 1999.

Latourette, Kenneth Scott. *The History of Early Relations Between the United States and China, 1784–1844*. New Haven, CT: Yale University Press, 1917.

Layton, Thomas N. *The Voyage of the Frolic*. Stanford, CA: Stanford University Press, 1997.

Lee, Jean Gordon. *Philadelphians and the China Trade, 1784–1844*. Philadelphia Museum of Art, 1984.

Leonard, D. L. *Missionary Annals of the Nineteenth Century*. Cleveland, OH: F.M. Barton, 1899.

Lew, Ling. *The Chinese in North America: A Guide to Their Life and Progress*. Los Angeles: East-West Culture Publishing, 1949.

Li, Chien-Nung. *The Political History of China, 1840–1928*. Princeton, NJ: D. Van Nostrand, 1956.

Lubbock, Basil. *The Coolie Ships and Oil Sailors*. Glasgow: Brown, Son & Ferguson, 1935

Lubbock, Basil. *The Opium Clippers*. Glasgow: Brown, Son & Ferguson, 1933.

MacMuellen, Jerry. *Paddle-Wheel Days in California*. Stanford, CA: Stanford University Press, 1944.

McKee, Delber L. *Chinese Exclusion Versus the Open Door Policy, 1900–1906*. Detroit: Wayne State University, 1977.

McKenzie, R. D. *Oriental Exclusion*. Chicago: University of Chicago, 1928.

McWilliams, Carey. *Brothers Under the Skin*. Boston: Little, Brown, 1943.

McWilliams, Carey. *Factories in the Field: The Story of Migratory Farm Labor in California*. Boston: Little, Brown, 1939.

Melendy, H. Brett and Benjamin F. Gilbert. *The Governors of California from Peter H. Burnett to Edmund G. Brown*. Georgetown, CA: Talisman Press, 1965.

Michael, Franz. *The Taiping Rebellion*, Vol. 1: *History*. Seattle: University of Washington Press, 1966.

O'Connor, Richard. *Pacific Destiny: An Informal History of the U.S. in the Far East*. Boston: Little, Brown, 1969.

Praetzellis, Mary and Adrian Praetzellis, et al. *Archaeological Research Design and Identification and Testing Strategies for Proposed Federal Courthouse Site,* *H156 Block, Sacramento, California*. Sonoma State University Academic Foundation, August 11, 1993.

Quincy, Josiah. *The Journals of Major Samuel Shaw*. Boston: Wm. Crosby and H. P. Nichols, 1847.

Reilly, Thomas H. *The Taiping Heavenly Kingdom Rebellion and the Blasphemy of Empire*. Seattle: University of Washington Press, 2004.

Ride, Lindsay and May Ride. *An East India Company Cemetery: Protestant Burials in Macao*. Hong Kong: Hong Kong University Press, 1996.

Roney, Frank. *Frank Roney: Irish Rebel and California Labor Leader*. Ed. Ira B. Cross. Berkeley: University of California Press, 1931.

Rubinstein, Murray A. *The Origins of the Anglo-American Missionary Enterprise in China, 1807–1840*. Lanham, MD: Scarecrow Press, 1996.

Sandmeyer, Elmer Clarence. *The Anti-Chinese Movement in California*. Urbana, IL: University of Illinois Press, reprint 1973.

Seward, George F. *Chinese Immigrants in Its Social and Economical Aspects*. New York: Charles Scribner's Sons, 1881.

Spence, Jonathan D. *Chinese Son, Heavenly Kingdom of Hong Xiuquan*. New York: W.W. Norton, 1996.

Stewart, Watt. *Chinese Bondage in Peru: A History of the Chinese Coolie in Peru, 1840*. Durham, NC: Duke University Press, 1951.

Swisher, Carl Brent. *Motivation and Political Technique in the California Constitutional Convention, 1878–79*. Claremont, CA: Pomona College, 1930.

The China Trade and Its Influences. New York: Metropolitan Museum of Art, 1941.

The Chinese in the Americas. New York: Overseas Chinese Culture Publishing, 1950.

Treat, Payson J. *The Far East: A Political and Diplomatic History*. New York: Harper & Brothers, 1928.

Neasham, V. Aubrey and James E. Henley. *The City of the Plain: Sacramento in the Nineteenth Century*. The Sacramento Pioneer Foundation, 1969.

Waley, Arthur. *The Opium War Through Chinese Eyes*. Stanford, CA: Stanford University Press, 1958.

Wheeler, L. N. *The Foreigner in China*. Chicago: S. C. Griggs, 1881.

Wong, Kin. *International Chinese Business Directory of the World, 1913*. International Chinese Business Directory Co.

Worden, Robert L. "A Chinese Reformer in Exile: The North American Phase of the Travels of K'ang Yu-wei, 1899–1909." Ph.D. dissertation, Georgetown University, 1972.

Yee, Alfred. *Shopping at Giant Foods: Chinese American Supermarkets in Northern California*. Seattle: University of Washington Press, 2003.

GOVERNMENT DOCUMENTS

Chinese Immigration: Its Social, Moral, and Political Effect. Report to the California State Senate of the Special Committee on Chinese Immigration. Sacramento State Office, 1878.

Hearing on Bigotry and Violence Against Asian Americans. Human Rights/Fair Housing Commission, City and County of Sacramento, May 17, 1984.

Sawyer, John B. Procedure on Section 6 and Other for Consular Offices. Washington: GPO, 1924.

State Board of Control of California. California and the Oriental: Japanese, Chinese, and Hindus. Sacramento: California State Printing Office, 1922.

The Immigrant Commission. Joint Commission on Immigration. Washington: GPO, 1911.

United States Bureau of the Census. Fifteenth Census of the United States: 1930.

United States Bureau of the Census. Fourteenth Census of the United States: 1940.

United States Bureau of the Census. Population Census. Microfilm from 1850 through 1920.

United States National Archives (Record groups to be added)

UNPUBLISHED SOURCES

Chinn, Florence J. *A Tree Growing in Gold Mountain.* Self-published book, 1996.

Chong, Lana Fong. Story of a Chinese Farmer in Sacramento Valley, 1920–1995. Manuscript in possession of Lana Chong.

Loo, Andrew Ben. Biography of 103 Centennarian Loo Lin. Manuscript in possession of Carol Jan Lee.

Lum, Margaret (Fong). Life as a Chinese American. Autobiography.

Yee, Franklin K. The History of Chinese Medicine in Sacramento. Manuscript in possession of Franklin Yee.

Yuen, Al. The Story of Owyang Hong Hing (Ah Hing, Pa Hing). Biography. Manuscript in possession of Hing Owyang.

Left to right: Geof Fong, Jeanie Lee, Rick Wong, Merlayna Yee-Chin, Frank Martinez, Joyce Eng, Karun Yee, Charlie May, Donna Scotti, Dr. Douglas Yee, Brenda Fong, David Young

THE CHINESE AMERICAN COUNCIL OF SACRAMENTO was established 20 years ago by Frank Fat to serve the needs of the Sacramento Chinese community and is committed to building a stronger Chinese-American presence through leadership in advocacy, civic and cultural activities. CACS has provided scholarships, school supplies, holiday gifts and disaster relief. As Sacramento's primary Chinese historical organization, CACS has produced author/ lecture dinners, Ethnic Village Gold Rush Days, museum exhibits in the Federal Courthouse and the Discovery Museum.

CACS board members have also served as advisors on the Ping Yuen and Locke developments. Many Asian leaders began their community service careers by serving on the CACS board. The Chinese American Council of Sacramento is proud to bring attention to the importance of the historical contributions of the Chinese people of Sacramento.

INDEX

Lum, Lien Ung, 85, 86
Lum, Margaret (Fong), 145
Lum, Nolan, 84, 86
Lum Goon, 84, 86
Lung, Billy Ho, 33

M

Mah Lien Ung, 86
Manchu (Qing) monarchy, xi, 9-10, 11, 12, 57
  overthrow of, 113-114, 115, 117
Manual of Procedures, 59
Marauders, 111
marriage, 83-84, 86, 88, 95
Marriott, Richard H., 127
Marsh, Mrs., 106
Marshall, John W., 39
Martila Communications Group, 139
Marysville, vii, ix
matchmakers, 84
McDougal, John, 40
McKim steamship, 19
medical practitioners, 22, 94, 116, 132-133
Meegan, Cheryl Chun, 136
M. E. Mission, 30
merchant immigration exemptions, 58-60
Methodist Chinese Mission, 106
migratory labor, 40
Miller, Tony, 67
Ming dynasty, 3
Minnick, Sylvia Suri, vii
Mint steamship, 19
Morrison Missionary School, 47
Morrison, Robert, 6, 10
Moulder, Andrew J., 132
Musical Mandarins, 100, 108

N

Nanking Treaty, 9, 10
National Alliance, 139
nationalism, overseas Chinese and, 110, 112, 115-117, 129
National Salvation League, Sacramento Chapter, 117
Native Americans, 68
New Life Movement, 117
newspaper publishing, 24, 25, 115, 145
New Way Market, 78
Ng, Linda, 145
Ngee-fauh, vii
Ning Yeung hui kuan, 90
nitroglycerine, 43
Non-Partisan Anti-Chinese Association, 52

O

one-stop shopping, 75
Ong, Sam, 127
Ong Ko Met Association, 90
Ono, Marion, 138
Open Door policy, 52
opera, 30

opium
  China trade and, xi, 7, 9, 11
  immigrant despair and, 86, 88
  war, 57
Oroville, vii
overseas Chinese *See wah que* (overseas Chinese)
Overseas Chinese of America, 145
Owyang, Helen (Fong), 88, 95, 131
Owyang, Hing, Jr., 95
Oy Ling Ranch, 69

P

Pacific Women's Golf Association (PWGA), 130
paper father and paper son, 58
Parker, Peter, 6
Patton, George, 123
Peace One Collective, 138
Pearl Harbor, 119, 123
Pearl River Delta, 12, 145
Pearl steamer, 24
People's Protective Alliance, 49
performing arts, 24, 30, 100
Perkins, George C., 52
Perry, Matthew, 57
philanthropists, 136
point stations, 60
political anti-Chinese actions, 47-52
political office holders, Chinese, 136
Pony Exchange, 33
porcelain, 3
poultry business, 88
poverty, 86, 88
Powderly, Terence V., 59
pre-investigation of status, 59
Presbyterian Mission, 106
Promontory Point, Utah, ix
Punti and Hakka feud, 12

Q

Qing monarchy See Manchu (Qing) monarchy
Quan, George, Jr., 78, 145
Quan, George Hong, 78, 83-84
Quan, Mary, 88
Que Lup Wah Gow Tong, 91
Quong Fung, 68-69, 71

R

railroad construction, ix, 39, 41, 43, 44
real estate covenants, 95
red egg and ginger party, 88, 95
Republic of China, 114, 115
retail food industry, 75-81
Roberts, Issachar J., 10
Roche, Robert E., 127
rococo style, 3
Russell, Samuel, 6
Russell, Sturgis and Company, 48